Y2K

W9-CCD-268

Y2K

An Action Plan to Protect
Yourself, Your Family,
Your Assets, and
Your Community on
January 1, 2000

VICTOR W. PORLIER

HarperCollins*Publishers*

This publication has been written to provide the author's opinions regarding the subject matter discussed. It is sold with the understanding that the author is not rendering legal, accounting, investment, health, medical, or any other professional service. If legal, accounting, investment, health, medical, or any other professional service is required, the services of a competent professional service provider should be sought.

The author specifically disclaims any personal liability for any loss or risk incurred as a consequence of the use and application, either directly or indirectly, of any advice or information presented herein.

Y2K. Copyright © 1999 by Victor W. Porlier. All rights reserved. Printed in the United States of America. No part of this book may be used or reproduced in any manner whatsoever without written permission except in the case of brief quotations embodied in critical articles and reviews. For information address HarperCollins Publishers, Inc., 10 East 53rd Street, New York, NY 10022.

HarperCollins books may be purchased for educational, business, or sales promotional use. For information please write to Special Markets Department, HarperCollins Publishers, Inc., 10 East 53rd Street, New York, NY 10022.

FIRST EDITION

Designed by Nancy Singer Olaguera

Library of Congress Cataloging-in-Publication Data available upon request.

ISBN 0–06–273675–2

99 00 01 02 ❖/RRD 10 9 8 7 6 5 4 3 2 1

Contents

Introduction

Quietly, invisibly, over the last forty years, the technological world has been heading for a *Titanic* moment. Back then, when computer memory was prohibitively expensive, the decision was made to economize on the date by using two digits instead of four for the year. This decision is now catching up with us. We don't know how automated systems will behave in the year 2000.

No, all the computers won't conk out at the stroke of midnight, January 1, 2000. But many will—there are billions and billions of chips and programs in use worldwide—and not enough time to check them all.

My purpose in writing this book is to alert my fellow citizens to the hazards ahead, to urge everyone to focus on *reducing the severity of the disaster.*

The linchpin of our industrialized world is electrical-power generation. If the electricity continues to be available, there's hope that everything else can be managed. If it fails, we are in deep trouble. Contact your government representatives on state and federal levels and urge that the functioning of our electrical systems be given the highest priority.

Then look to your own backyard. Every single person who makes prudent preparation for the crisis will be helping everyone else. Every single person who sets aside supplies and is ready to assist others will be an important agent in our recovery from an unprecedented technological breakdown.

Victor Porlier
January 1999

PART I

What's Y2K All About?

It's a stunning fact that two small digits have the potential for setting the world on its ear. There are billions of computer chips out there and billions of lines of computer codes that must be reviewed before the year 2000. No one knows where the glitches will be, and there isn't enough time left for remediation to be completed.

CHAPTER 1

What Does Y2K Mean?

It's the short way of saying the year 2000 (*Y* stands for *year*, and *K* is an abbreviation for *thousand*). In the early years of computers, data storage space was at a premium. To save space, the 19 was left off the year, so that a date such as April 15, 1998, is recorded as 04/15/98. On January 1, 2000, the date will come up as 01/01/00, which many computers will read as an error. When that happens, an unknown number of computer systems—certainly a great many—will stop working or will work erratically.

Why are dates so important? Dates trigger a multitude of events—startups, shutdowns, deliveries, billing, inventory replacement, and so on. Dates are essential in determining age eligibilities and in carrying out financial transactions. Interest rates are highly date-sensitive. Embedded dates for comparisons and calculations are found in and flowing through computers, telecommunications, microwave transmitters, satellites, and all manner of electromechanical devices upon which our lives and economy depend.

Didn't anyone foresee this problem? Why was the decision made to express the year in only two digits? A good question. One that leads back to the late fifties and early sixties, when there were no inexpensive mass storage devices. Data were stored on punched paper cards and magnetic tape, with the core memory stored in the mainframe.

In 1970, when one megabyte of internal computer memory (RAM) cost $3.2 million (contrasted with today's cost of $5 for a megabyte of RAM and about ten cents for disc memory) it made sense to economize memory in any way possible. Saving just two digits by leaving out the 19 in the year entry field seemed a reasonable tradeoff at the time.

The two-digit date was never fixed. As hardware improved, access to data in existing applications and databases was essential, but no one wanted to incur the major costs that deep renovations—such as changing all the dates—would require. So the two-digit format for rendering the year was carried forward to ensure compatibility year after year; emerging improvements in hardware and software could be implemented more cheaply and quickly, and with fewer coding errors.

Forty years into this process, we have countless computer platforms and software languages around the world, and systems with billions and billions of lines of code with the two-digit-year fields embedded in them. The two-digit year also crept into the microchips used in health-care devices, industrial processes, military defense, and so on.

The obvious solution. Why not just replace all the two-digit codes and chips with ones that express the year in four digits? The problem is finding them. "Legacy" systems—those that have been in place for decades—are deeply embedded in most of our present major systems. They are frequently undocumented; the source codes often are lost; many early computer languages and coding techniques are indecipherable today; and the original programmers are mostly retired or dead.

A glitch that's hard to track. In cases where early computer systems have been modernized, date-sensitive chips might remain. In some instances, they might be in places that are physically difficult to reach (consider the computer chips in an offshore drilling rig).

Why not buy all new equipment? Easier said than done—or afforded. The systems that run, say, a modern municipal waterworks are not just sitting on a shelf in a store somewhere. To perform tasks of any complexity, computers have to be programmed by experts. If you have ever been around a new computer installation, you know that this can take months, even years.

Even new equipment may not work. A little-discussed fact of computer construction is the casual way in which chips are handled. Unless great caution is exercised, an old computer chip can easily find its way into a new device. So even new equipment must be tested before January 1, 2000, to be sure that "new" is really entirely new.

Will there be a "silver bullet"? "They," the computer scientists, have been searching for the one-size-fits-all solution for years. Given the enormous variety of computers, software, and embedded systems, it isn't even theoretically possible that one solution could fit all. The bottom line is this: there's too much to fix and too little time in which to do it all.

CHAPTER 2

This Is Not a Drill

There's general agreement that when the year 2000 arrives, many, many computers will shut down, causing power outages, breakdowns in communications, and a host of other problems. Traditionally, when one part of the country has a flood or hurricane damage, the rest of the nation comes to the rescue. This time, no region is likely be untouched, so we can't count on a cavalry coming to the rescue. Everyone is going to have to look locally to find help—and to give help.

But before we go into the ramifications of Y2K troubles, consider these points:

Don't let's panic. The human condition has always been fraught with danger, and those people who get through hard times best are those who keep their wits about them.

Batten the hatches. There's still time to make sensible moves to prepare for this ride we're all about to take into the unknown. We don't have Joseph's biblical seven years, but we do have—at this writing—about 12 months to make preparations. This book is intended to help you set your own personal priorities and get started on your own plans to protect yourself, your family, your friends, and your community from civil disorders.

The government needs to hear from you. Government officials on the federal, state, county, city, and all other levels need to hear from us: The Electorate. Ask where they stand on Y2K plans and progress, and demand straight answers. You'll learn here why it's not enough to ask if repair is going forward (it's called remediation). And why "It's being taken care of" is not a satisfactory answer. It's also essential to ask if all the systems and their interconnections among government levels are being *tested*. How are they being tested and what are the deadlines?

Sweet are the uses of adversity. It may help to think of this impending crisis as a chance to get back to basics. People pay good money to go off and learn wilderness survival skills, to pit themselves against nature, adversity, and so forth. Well, here's a free course in the offing, and it may even have some pluses to it. It can give you a new view of the basics of your life, both in possessions and in thinking. What's really important? What can go into the discard and good riddance?

CHAPTER 3

Like It or Not, We're Computer-Dependent

It is impossible to overstate how much our lives are governed by computers. The utilities upon which we depend are totally computerized. Electrical power in the lower forty-eight states is provided by more than seven thousand enterprises (public and private) that generate and/or sell electricity. They are all on a common, interconnected grid of four major regions that reach into Canada. This grid system is designed to share power and also to protect against a spreading blackout.

A few power outages can be managed. These gargantuan power grids are designed for flexibility. What they can't manage will be widespread power outages, especially since some of the glitches will be extremely difficult to track and fix. During the famous Northeast blackout of 1965, the phone systems functioned very well in that short period, providing reassurance to all concerned. The reason was that the phone companies had reserve generators and battery-operated backup systems. When Y2K hits, we'll be lucky if the phones do as well.

Computer failure will endanger health. We take for granted our wonderful water supplies: pure drinking water, flushing toilets, and showers. But most water systems, too, are run by computer, as are our police and fire departments, our hospitals, and our transportation systems.

Food supplies will be jeopardized. Supermarkets and grocery stores are heavily computerized. At the supermarket, when the bar code on your jar of peanut butter is passed over the laser at the checkout counter, an automatic order goes to the producer to replace it. But this system might break down, the checkout counter itself may not work, and, for that matter, the cash register might conk out.

In any case, most supermarkets have only a three days' supply of food on their shelves. If there are massive power failures (among the producers and the transporting companies), there is a very real danger of food shortages. The typical food item travels 1,300 miles before it gets to your table. Many others come from much, much farther away.

Delayed Social Security and Medicare checks. Almost all governmental activities—federal, state, and city—are totally computerized, including the generation of Social Security checks and Medicare payments and a wide array of government entitlements. (See page 57 for where we stand on this.)

Business troubles. Most businesses, large and small, use computers at almost every stage in their production. Even if an individual company gets its computers in order ("Y2K-compliant" is the term), business as usual might still prove impossible. Everything from traffic lights to the air-traffic control system will be at risk. When the Galaxy IV satellite acted up in May 1998, America's 45 million pagers and other telecommunications couldn't function. This skip in our technological heartbeat gave us a warning and a preview of things to come.

The personal level. There may be too many glitches at your company for you to continue to work. You may face a layoff or the loss of a job. So it's not just your own PC or your TV that is at risk on January 1, 2000—it's the whole world in which we live.

CHAPTER 4

Why Aren't More People Worried About Y2K?

Government officials, business leaders, and the general public have been amazingly oblivious of the impending Y2K disaster. Setting aside the fact that politicians are notoriously reluctant to be the bearers of bad news, there are several obstacles to the public's gaining a general knowledge of this situation.

Media coverage has been poor. Most people—even our political leaders—rely on TV for the news. TV and radio have always broadcast warnings of hurricanes, floods, tornadoes, forest fires, and the like. We have come to accept their priorities as our own, but, except for a few reports on CSPAN, CBN, CNN, and ABC (as of this writing), TV has given Y2K short shrift. Most print media have provided no more than occasional bits and pieces about Y2K. Only after President Clinton's long overdue speech on July 14, 1998, and a front-page report in *The New York Times* on July 12, 1998, about Wall Street's initial Y2K tests, did the issue get brief coverage by both *The Today Show* and Dan Rather. Finally, on August 2, 1998, *The New York Times*, the nation's leading newspaper, acknowledged in a belated editorial the crippling potential of the Millennium Bug.

We're used to trusting authority. People have faith in the federal government, in central banks, and in business in general. We believe that monetary and fiscal tools have all but insured us against an economic contraction comparable to the Depression of the thirties. The unprecedented pervasiveness of computer-chip breakdown—and the magnitude of possible economic consequences—is beyond the imaginations of most nontechnical people.

Resistance to bad news. We are a nation of pragmatic optimists, pretty much sold on the power of positive thinking. We believe that if we set our minds to do something (in this case, weather an epidemic of computer glitches), it's a done deal.

Disbelief in dire warnings. People tend to regard warnings of disaster as just so much rhetoric—a case of crying wolf. Remember the population explosion that was supposed to cause mass starvation? The 1973 oil embargo that was supposed to leave us all cold and in the dark? We have had so many warnings of ecological catastrophes that never came to pass that people are not inclined to take any warnings seriously.

How bad can it get? People's experience with floods, tornadoes, hurricanes, earthquakes, and power outages all suggests that, however horrendous the event, we have the resources and experts—National Guard, electricians, and so on— to set things right. The popular faith is that eventually everything gets fixed.

It's too complicated. For most people computer systems are a complete mystery. Technical problems, often discussed in terms of "bugs" and "debugging," are perceived as simple, singular problems. People do not grasp the interconnected complexity of our technological world. They don't realize that when the day comes, it's not going to be a matter of just getting the TV fixed or not being able to phone others to find out if they are all right. It's likely to determine whether they can get money out of the ATM. Indeed, because food deliveries to stores are heavily dependent on computers, there's a possibility of widespread, long-term food shortages.

CHAPTER 5

What Do Business, Industry, and Government Need to Do?

The severity of the year 2000 crisis will depend largely upon the extent to which government, business, industry, and individual enterprises act quickly and effectively, committing time and resources to review, update, and test in these five areas:

1. **Update computer hardware and software systems.** Updates are needed in both the systems that control *administration* (for example the recording of your Social Security and tax payments) and the systems that control *operations* (the sending out of Social Security checks and the generating of electricity). It's not just mainframes that must be checked—desktop PCs, client server systems, and companywide telecoms are also vulnerable.

2. **Find and replace date-sensitive chips in embedded systems.** The concern here is the kinds of chips that will quit working when the year 2000 comes up. There are millions—make that billions—of chips in play, so the task is stupendous. One company attempted to get around the Y2K problem by

14

buying all new PCs. When they tested the new computers, 17 percent of them failed. Why? The machines were new, but some contained old, non-Y2K-compliant chips. This is a pervasive computer problem—the vast number of old chips that find their way into new equipment.

3. **Determine the status of compliance along the chain.** It's not enough for individual companies to fix their own computer systems. They've got to check out their connections with others. Are suppliers going to be able to provide the goods and services that are needed? Are customers going to be able to continue to buy goods and services? Will banks be able to handle the transactions?

4. **Test crucial electronic data interchanges** in both business and governmental entities. Computers run security and safety alarms—not just for buildings and critical systems, but for hazardous materials as well. For example, your phone company's 911 service is connected electronically to the local police, fire, and emergency medical departments. Have these connections been fully tested? If not, what is the timetable for their testing?

5. **Develop contingency plans** for providing services if a particular system fails. Obviously, some systems will be easier to fix than others. But diagnosis of a breakdown can take months. What is the organization's fallback position if downtime is prolonged? Bear in mind that computers have been in use for so long that there are some systems without any equivalent manual backup system.

An example of this is our vast railroad system, which transports all manner of goods, especially fuels and chemicals. My uncle, who is a recently retired railroad yardman, says that most of the old manual switching gear in the yards has been ripped out. Computerized switching systems are now the only way to move freight.

We can't go back to old ways of doing business. Except for a very few small-scale operations, we can't just "roll up our sleeves and get the job done." It would be physically impossible to accomplish by hand what computers do in the area of, say, medical testing or international monetary transactions. Senator Robert Bennett, Republican of Utah, put it this way in speaking at the National Press Club in Washington, D.C., on July 15, 1998:

> *We cannot go back because the infrastructure that under-girded our entire society twenty-five years ago has been dismantled. It is gone. The skills are gone, the people are gone, the equipment is gone. Like it or not, we have no choice in this situation but to plow forward and, one way or another, make it work . . . .*

CHAPTER 6

"Our People Are Working on It"

Do you believe this? We all like to be reassured. We prefer to think that everything is under control. But when it comes to Y2K compliance, platitudes won't do. What is at issue is continuity of utilities, the functioning of the workplace (your job), and civil order. The security of your assets is at stake—what you have in the bank, in stocks, in bonds, and in other investments. You have a right to know whether or not your assets are protected from loss.

Don't just hope for the best. It is up to the able-bodied among us to look after our family's safety, physical and financial. It is also up to the able to care for the aged and infirm. Will utilities continue to function on January 1, 2000? Will the lights work? How about the water supply? Will fuel supplies come through? We have had some remarkably mild winters of late. However, we can't count on the weather not to be cold—perhaps brutally cold—when this memorable New Year arrives.

Ask for a status report. Undoubtedly, in financial institutions of all kinds, people are working on the Y2K problem. What you need to know is where they stand. We need to jog a great number of people out of their fog. Farther along you will find a list of questions to ask the key players in our highly interactive world. (See page 91 for more on this topic.)

Get it in writing. If you call to find out where, say, your bank is in the remediation (upgrading) process, be sure to ask for a letter confirming the substance of your conversation. If you decide to put your queries in writing (see page 95) be sure to send the letter by certified mail, with a return receipt requested. This way, the organization cannot deny that it received your questions.

Get the word out. Once people are convinced that there is a Y2K crisis, generally their first response is, "What can I do? Whom should I write to?" It is clear that there are many willing helpers out there just waiting to be enlisted in the fight to get preparedness plans underway while there is still time to act. Find out if there is a community activist group near you. If so, join it; if not, start one yourself. (See page 25 for more on this topic.)

CHAPTER 7

How Do We Know This Isn't Chicken Little Revisited?

In the fine old tradition of shooting the messenger who brings bad news, many in the media have been giving the Y2K spokesmen quite a drubbing. One critic has gone so far as to say that talk about the Y2K problem is "the biggest fraud perpetrated by consultants on the business community since re-engineering." Whoa! First, consider this: at most, Y2K consultants are earning fees for their services—hardly a massive rip-off. Second, it is imbecilic to suppose that distinguished computer specialists, economists, engineers, scientists, and politicians would risk their reputations issuing warnings if the situation didn't warrant it. They, better than anyone else, know that the moment of truth is very near. In fact, it's only about a year away.

Y2K is, at root, technological. And there already have been many manifestations of the problem. For example, *The New York Post* recently reported the following:

> *A large retailer was surprised when its computerized inventory management and pricing system put an entire*

shipment of brand new goods on deep discount when they had not been on the store's shelves for more than a day. A savvy manager discovered the problem. The store regularly programmed its bar code readers to discount a product that had not sold for 21 months. But because 21 months from now is the year 2000, the system became confused and, assuming these products had been sitting around since 1900, slashed their prices.

Some critics have tried to downgrade the Y2K threat as a foolish case of "millennium fever." (This "fever," a kind of hysteria, was said to have struck the populace a thousand years ago. True, there were some few who expected spiritual signs and wonders at the year 1000—perhaps the return of Christ. But it is highly unlikely that people sat up on December 31 in the year 999 fearing the arrival of the year 1000, especially given the imprecision of ancient calendars.

Y2K is not an alien plot. Nor does it have anything to do with cosmic rays, UFOs, or sci-fi plots. Nothing could be further from the truth—there is nothing spooky or supernatural about a rash of crashing computers. On August 2, 1998, *The New York Times* acknowledged in their editorial, "The Millennium Bug Looms,"

The breakdowns could be minor, or they could disable everything from air traffic control systems to financial networks, powergrids, hospitals and home appliances. Some economists warn of a global recession. It makes sense to prepare for the worst.

CHAPTER 8

How Long Are Computer Dislocations Likely to Last?

No one knows, but the prudent person should make preparations to weather at least two to four weeks of electrical blackouts, and three to eighteen months of sporadic outages, shortages, and unexpected complications. Bear in mind that the problem will strike in midwinter in the northern hemisphere, and snow and sleet may add to other difficulties. The next solar flare cycle will be getting underway in 2000, and history shows that such flares affect satellites, telemetry, and the generation of electricity.

Y2K threatens a real domino effect. Modern commerce is so highly interconnected that a failure in one place can trigger chains of failures. For example, in August 1997, workers in a single company, United Parcel Service, went on strike. They were out for only 15 days, but this relatively brief interruption of service resulted in hundreds of bankruptcies. Many companies have come to rely on just-in-time delivery, which saves on inventory and storage. What happens when there's no delivery? No work, no product, no income. Many small and not-so-small companies are vulnerable because they operate on a thin margin of profit.

It's not just weak companies that will suffer. Strong companies can go under in times of business stress. Unemployment in one sector can adversely affect many others. For example, travel and recreational industries, which are robust at the moment, can expect a severe contraction if there are widespread layoffs throughout the country.

What about the rest of the world? This is an urgent question, as the economic health of the United States is intertwined with the economies of Europe, Asia, Latin America, and Africa. In Europe computer specialists have been preoccupied with the computer programming necessary to implement the changeover to the Euro, all to the detriment of Y2K remediation. In Asia, where there have been currency devaluations, recessions, and natural disasters (such as catastrophic forest fires of Indonesia), attention and resources have been diverted from Y2K remediation.

Global Y2K awareness lags. Worldwide recognition of the Y2K problem has been hampered by the fact that many non-European countries have other cultural and religious calendars that are of far greater significance to their people than the Gregorian calendar, which they use only in business. This compounds the problem of trying to develop an awareness of the Y2K crisis. The year 2000 is not the kind of historical marker, say, in Japan or Korea that it is for us.

As of this writing, we are experiencing a worldwide economic contraction. Unfortunately, this means there will be far too little attention to the ramifications of computer breakdowns internationally.

PART II

Your Y2K Action Plans

In many parts of the country people know what it is to prepare for a hurricane or rising floodwaters. This time, we're all in the same boat—we may or may not be hit by power outages or specific glitches. If you and your family make preparations now for a period of suspended services, you'll be that much safer for the year 2000—and, of course, if there's a hurricane.

CHAPTER 9

A Plan for Y2K Emergencies

Hurricanes, floods, and severe snowstorms occur somewhere in this country every year. And every year emergency groups on local, state, and federal levels—aided by the Red Cross, the Salvation Army, and others—swing into action, rescuing disaster victims and providing basic necessities.

Y2K poses a new kind of threat. Its effects—power outages and loss of water, heat, and communication—could easily occur *simultaneously* over the entire country or in a large number of areas. So we may not have the familiar circumstance of an afflicted region—say the Mississippi with floods—getting immediate help from other parts of the country. In a Y2K crisis, there will be few unaffected sections. Every region is likely to be isolated, each with emergencies of its own.

Create a survival plan. Tailor a survival strategy to your family and locale. You can start by calling a family conference to discuss what you will need to do. (What you will need in the way of specific supplies is covered in later sections of this book.) Make sure your children are included in the effort. It's important for them to know that their parents are responding—this makes them feel safe. But it is equally important that the children, as part of the family, have specific roles to perform. Discuss these roles at a family meeting.

For younger children, this exercise can be presented as an adventure in living like a pioneer family or as living the way the early colonists did.

Do a trial run. To get a vivid picture of what you'll be up against, set aside one family evening with no electric light, no TV, and no computer. With no gas or electric cooking possible, you will be eating cold food. (It's likely to give you a whole new appreciation of the kind of trail food carried by campers.) Also, avoid using the faucets. (There's no point to restricting use of the toilet during this drill because, in a real emergency, you may have to dispose of wastes by other means. Such waste disposal is discussed on page 49.)

Identify your local emergency agencies. Find out who is running the key organizations and what plans they have in place. For example, how would you be warned in case of emergency? Will there be emergency shelters? And will there be pre-positioned food, water, fuel, and emergency power generation? Where will they be located, and how will they be staffed? Will there be special assistance for elderly or disabled persons?

Schools and work. Inquire about their emergency-preparedness plans at schools, day-care centers, and at your job. If the work you do is vital to community survival (as for example, if you are a nurse, fireman, or police officer) and you will be expected to be on duty, it is even more important that your family have a plan of action.

Take the initiative. If no emergency plans are in place in any of the organizations you contact, urge that this issue be addressed at once. You can give force to your request by volunteering your help.

Draw a floor plan of your home. Show windows, doors, porch roofs, and so on. Mark two escape routes from each room. Discuss what to do in case of fire. Do your children know how to use a fire escape? If electricity fails, within a couple of weeks or less many water systems will have insufficient water pressure for firefighting.

Designate a place outside the home where household members should meet. This will prevent anyone's going back to look for someone who has already escaped. Practice emergency evacuation drills with all household members, stressing speed. (Y2K aside, this is something you should do twice a year.)

How will you get in touch? Make a plan for establishing emergency contact with other family members and friends in your area. Decide on rendezvous points. Will your children know where to go if they can't get back home? To whose home or what location (school, church, and so on) should they go? Children should routinely wear or carry whistles to signal for help.

Provide for your pets. This means including their food and water requirements in your plans. If for any reason you must evacuate your home, the Humane Society urges that you take your pets with you. Since emergency shelters will not accept animals (except ones that assist the disabled, such as seeing-eye dogs), you will have to make provisions for your pets elsewhere. Ask friends and relatives outside your area if they can shelter your pets in an emergency. Call kennels, hotels, and motels—again outside your immediate area—to find possible accommodations. For more information, contact the Humane Society of the United States, Disaster Services, 2100L Street, NW, Washington, DC 20037.

CHAPTER 10

Where Will You and Your Family Be?

The impact of Y2K on you and your family will vary from place to place, but generally speaking, smaller and medium-sized communities will probably fare better than high-density cities. For one thing, the higher the demand on the electrical supply, the more likely that there will be brownouts or blackouts.

Another consideration is that in times of shortage, the competition for goods and services—and its intensity—will be directly proportional to the numbers of people pursuing them. Thus it's probably better to be where there are fewer people.

Summer residences. If you have a cabin in the woods or some other getaway spot, you might consider stocking up on supplies and going there to usher in the year 2000. Perhaps, if you have family or friends who live in a more rural area, you might ask if they are willing to have you visit over the 1999–2000 holidays. If you do this, offer to pay for your own provisions. Or if you have been thinking of moving to a smaller town, now might would be a good time to act on the idea.

Safeguarding your home. Here are a number of things you can do to your existing home to make it safer and more livable during a crisis:

1. **Get to know your neighbors.** People who know each other can band together for, mutual support, common defense, and help in providing basic needs. You'll be safer in a group than on your own.

2. **Install dead-bolts** on your doors and make sure all your windows have working locks.

3. **Learn to defend yourself** in a manner that suits your personal values. This does not necessarily mean you have to have a gun if you are not comfortable in doing so. There are alternatives. If you decide to acquire a firearm, you must get training in its use and safety techniques.

4. **Modify your fireplace** (if you have one) to make it a more efficient source of heat. Or, if you have the right kind of space for it (a concrete, ceramic tile, or stone floor plus adequate ventilation), you might consider buying a wood-burning stove. These stoves, which are available in a wide variety of styles, are attractive and functional. If you do buy a wood-burning stove, get one with a surface that will allow you to cook at least one or two things—boil water, cook eggs, and so on. (For Products and Services, see page 157.) If you decide to buy a generator, the key decision is the fuel. (See page 33 for comparisons of gasoline, diesel, and propane fuels.)

CHAPTER 11

Apartment Buildings— Vertical Villages

Many systems in apartment buildings are automated—that is, they are run by computers: lights, intercom, elevators, boiler, ventilation, trash compactor, sprinkler system, security systems, and more. If any of these systems fail, repair is the responsibility of the owner of the building or the managing agent. Now would be a good time to ask about the status of your building. Are its major systems Y2K-compliant?

In theory, a breakdown is the owner's problem. But in fact, any breakdown is very much *your* problem. Especially if, all around, other apartment buildings are having the same problems and the repair people are impossible to reach.

Past experience with doorman strikes, garbage strikes, and the like have provided many apartment dwellers with valuable experience. The key to successful management of a crisis is the formation of a committee made up of unit owners or renters, who will hold meetings and set up contingency plans. A plan should be made—possibly a sign-up sheet—for apartment dwellers to staff the door if the doormen or other service people can't get to work.

Garbage needs tending. This is an important health issue. The committee should post regulations on every floor and in the elevators as to how garbage will be managed. This is a tough job and will need many people to pitch in. A first step is to seal off the chutes leading to the compactor. If the trash compactors aren't working, the debris will pile up and attract vermin. Tenants should bring only their moist garbage (wrapped as tightly as possible in plastic) and deposit it in heavy-duty black plastic bags in the basement. All recyclable material—newspapers, cans, glass, and plastic—should be kept in individual apartments until further notice.

What if the halls are dark? Nothing is darker than an inside corridor with the lights off. Is there a backup lighting system of the kind used in aircraft? Obviously, each tenant should have flashlights, a large supply of batteries (preferably the rechargeable NiCad type), and battery-operated electric Coleman lanterns (which are preferable to propane or kerosene).

Elevator failure threatens the elderly and the disabled. The committee should identify those who will need help. It can be assumed that delivery of some services from supermarkets and drugstores will be curtailed, so arrangements should be made to help the stranded get their groceries and medications and mail—assuming there is any.

CHAPTER 12

Light and Heat

Nuclear power plants (108) provide 22 percent of the nation's electric power. In the Northeast, the percentage is 40 percent. If any nuclear plant is closed down by the Nuclear Regulatory Commission because of safety concerns (to avoid nuclear accidents such as the Chernobyl experience), the remaining hydroelectric and fossil-fuel generating plants in the area will not be able to generate sufficient power for the region. We can then expect blackouts and rolling brownouts. Of course, if the nonnuclear plants are crippled by their own Y2K problems, the situation will be dire, indeed.

Electrical grid failure. If there is loss of power in one part of a grid, it can trigger losses and shutdowns in adjacent facilities. It's reasonable to assume that the power will go out in many locations. Here's what to consider before the power goes down:

1. **If you buy a generator, have it installed by a professional.** Get advice on where to put it and how to store fuel. The second issue is the choice of fuel. Propane lasts indefinitely, and is clean; a propane-powered generator is better because it uses the most desirable fuel. By contrast, gasoline is a short-term

fuel (assuming that you will be able to get it) that will begin to go stale after thirty days. Additives can extend its useful life somewhat. The octane declines over time, but for some engines it can be used for several months. Diesel fuel lasts much longer, but its fumes are very strong, and diesel generators are very noisy. Yet they are stable workhorses with few breakdowns and may be the best choice for certain settings.

2. **Check your ventilation,** especially if you are using any kind of heating, particularly a fireplace. A house that is too well sealed can be hazardous. It's better to be a bit cold than to suffocate.

3. **Lay in a supply of candles**—the more the better. Beeswax candles are dripless and long-burning, but relatively expensive. A better choice would be the long-burning votive candles usually available in grocery stores; votives may last up to twenty-four hours. Avoid scented candles if anyone in the group has allergies. But there are some benefits to having candles that purify the air, such as Pure Magic by Faroy.

4. **To light up, buy waterproof matches** at a camping supply store. Failing that, try the old Girl Scout trick of waterproofing ordinary wooden matches with clear nail polish. And get a supply of cheap lighters—you can buy a bundle of Bic lighters for a modest price.

5. **Coleman lanterns come in many sizes** and give light that is steady enough to read by. However, a large Coleman Northstar Electric Lantern using 8 D-cell alkaline batteries can supply light at its highest setting for only eight hours.

6. **You could invest in a battery recharger,** but the catch here is that you have to recharge alkalines before they are 50 percent depleted. A better solution is the purchase of the more expensive NiCad batteries. Because NiCads can be run down to nothing and still be recharged again and again, they are a good choice for your flashlights and battery-operated radios as well. Obviously, the recharger requires electricity. In the case of sporadic outages, you'll have to recharge whenever the electricity is on. As an alternative, solar-panel rechargers are available.

7. **Reduce your use of electricity** in times of crisis. It makes sense to conserve as much as you can and urge others to do so as well. And, on the eve of the year 2000, it would make sense to unplug a few things—especially your major appliances and your computer for a few hours. This may protect equipment from any irregularities in the flow of electricity, such as sudden power surges. (See the checklist on page 124 for more about lighting and heating products.)

CHAPTER 13

Your Water Supply Is of the First Importance

You can live without a lot of things, but water isn't one of them. People can die after only a few days without water. The generally accepted rule of thumb is that you need to provide at least a gallon of water per person per day. Half is for drinking, and half is for bathing, washing dishes, and flushing toilets. Some even urge two gallons a day. (Use paper products and forget dishwashing for the moment.) The recommended way to purify water is to boil it for at least ten minutes.

Stock up on bottled water. Use 2.5-liter containers. Or you can empty clean soda bottles (2-liter size), fill them with tapwater, and add four to six drops of unscented chlorine bleach to each; the water will keep indefinitely if stored in a cool, dry place. Alternatively, the water can be cleansed with iodine tablets, which you can get at drug or camping stores. (Warning: some people are allergic to iodine.) To mask the taste of iodine, you can use powdered drink mixes. Don't use milk cartons or flimsy containers that are designed to degrade. Try to keep at least a two weeks' supply on hand at all times. Emergency preparedness people suggest at least a month's supply, but that could be problematic for people with limited space.

Outdoor sources of water. If you have a pond or stream or some other outside water source, all the better. But make sure you have a decent water filter to run it through before use. The Katadyn water filters, which are popular with hikers and campers, would be good for this purpose. If you have an electric-powered well, a backup for its use would be a hand pump if the well is within forty feet of the surface. A backup generator may be essential. Or you might explore a solar-powered water pump (sold at Real Goods). You might want to look into solar-powered or wind-powered options to keep the well operational.

You can always collect rainwater in barrels, in clean, fifty-five-gallon drums or wooden buckets. Preferably, use containers that have never had anything else in them. Garbage pails that have ever actually been used for garbage should only be used as a last resort, after a thorough cleansing.

CHAPTER 14

Lay in Food Supplies Now

What's the difference between stockpiling and hoarding? It's all in the timing. If you lay up reserve supplies now, you may be able to protect yourself and your family from privation in the future. And setting some food aside for neighbors who didn't prepare is wise on several counts. Once a crisis hits, it is clearly too late to stockpile. Then it's likely to be a matter of just getting by.

In instances of long-term shortages and shutdowns, government agencies will probably institute rationing systems. And, of course, rationing usually carries sanctions against hoarding.

Rural dwellers are used to stockpiling food and other supplies because of the distances to stores and because power outages and severe winters are a fact of country living. For those who live on farms or out in the country, it may just be a matter of checking to be sure that you have an adequate supply of necessities for a longer term than usual.

Conveniently located supermarkets have caused many people to depend on weekly and even daily shopping. So planning for a month's or even two months' necessities for the whole family seem a serious hardship—especially if you loathe list-making. To commandeer the space necessary for bulky supplies such as bottled water, paper towels, toilet paper, canned goods, plastic garbage bags, dog food, kitty litter, and so on, take a good look at your closets, garage, basement, attic, and any spare rooms; make use of space under beds and nooks or crannies.

Apartment dwellers are at a disadvantage, having the least space and the greatest risk of food shortages. After shelter, the highest priority is water. Apartment dwellers should seek to stock foods that are extremely compact, such as the dehydrated packaged meals routinely used by campers. For more about this topic, see page 44.)

Not everyone lives near a warehouse store (Sam's, Costco, or a BJ's), where huge quantities of essentials can be acquired at relatively low cost. Food prices vary regionally (and seasonally), so it's not possible to talk about how much you will have to spend to prepare for contingencies.

What about the expiration dates on food? Obviously, foods with a short shelf life (say a week or two) are not suitable for stockpiling. There are many differing opinions about how long canned goods can be safely stored. We follow the advice of my wife's favorite food retailer, Wegman's, that has helpfully provided the following on the Internet:

"In general, most canned goods have a long 'health life,' and when properly stored are safe to eat for several years.

- Low-acid canned goods—2 to 5 years (canned meat and poultry, stews, soups except tomato, pasta products, potatoes, corn, carrots, spinach, beans, beets, peas, and pumpkin).

- High-acid canned goods—12 to 18 months (tomato products, fruits, sauerkraut, and foods in vinegar-based sauces or dressings).

- Some canned hams are shelf-stable. But do not store ham or any foods labeled 'keep refrigerated' in the pantry. Such foods must be stored in the refrigerator.

- Shelf-stable foods such as canned goods, cereal, baking mixes, pasta, dry beans, mustard, and ketchup can be kept safely at room temperature.

- To keep these foods at their best quality, store in clean, dry, cool (in below-85°F cabinets, away from the stove or exhaust from the refrigerator).

- Extremely hot (over 100°F) and cold temperatures are harmful to canned goods.

- Never use food from cans that are leaking, bulging, badly dented, or with a foul odor; cracked jars or jars with loose or bulging lids; or any container that spurts liquid when you open it. Never taste such foods. Throw out any food you suspect is spoiled."

Freeze-dried and dehydrated foods are long-lasting. If purchased now, they will be perfectly fine and nutritious into the next century. Sporting-goods stores often carry such meals for campers. Unprocessed grains and dried beans are durable staples. Look for foods that require no preparation or as little as possible, such as "add water." And if heat is unavailable, it's a good idea to stock foods that can be eaten without having to be cooked or reconstituted.

Forget frozen foods as emergency supplies. When the power goes off, frozen foods begin to defrost and deteriorate. A couple of days is as long as such food will last. Some people will be able to store foods outside if the weather is freezing, but it wouldn't do to invest hundreds of dollars in frozen goods on the chance that the weather will cooperate.

Stockpiling is a good long-term habit. The rule is store what you eat and eat what you store. After Y2K has played itself out, you might think about continuing the drill; there's no way of knowing when your region will be hit by power outages, storms, and so forth. If you have a six months' supply of food on hand for each person in your family (with some for your neighbors and some possibly to use in barter), you need only replenish the larder, not start from scratch.

Most of the foods you will be stockpiling are the items you would normally use, with the exception of powdered milk and powdered eggs. It's a way of ensuring self-sufficiency.

Garbage bags are unsuitable for storing anything edible because they are often treated with insecticides. Avoid all but bags marked specifically for food storage.

What about growing your own food? During World War II, people planted what were called Victory Gardens, some 20 million of them nationwide. So successful were they that by the end of 1943, these gardens had produced an estimated 40 percent of all vegetables consumed. If you have the space and the inclination to try gardening, get started now. Many gardening books are available with the basics. (We provide a beginner's checklist of tools on page 138.)

Plant only nonhybrid vegetable seeds, which reproduce themselves as hybrids cannot. These can be obtained from a variety of outlets. (See our Products and services section on page 157 for a list of nonhybrid seed companies.) State agricultural services can tell you what will grow in your area and can provide other regional advisories (soil conditions and so forth). See the Blue Pages in your phone book for state government listings.

CHAPTER 15

Nutritionally Wise Choices

Maintaining high energy levels and a healthy immune system at times of extreme stress means that your body must get what it needs. Most programs for long-term food-storage emphasize the importance of carbohydrates and advise storing large quantities of grains, usually wheat. But this one-size-fits-all approach may be detrimental to some people. Here are some points to keep in mind:

For people who have food allergies, stockpile alternative foods: soy or rice milk instead of cow's milk, rice for potatoes, spelt for wheat. Leavened bread is not good for those intolerant to yeast.

Those following specific regimens, such as the D'Adamo blood type diet, will need to stockpile those foods that are listed in his book as highly beneficial for their family's blood types. People following the Atkins diet should think about having sufficient supplies of protein and the recommended high-protein snacks on hand. It would be wise to order these supplies early.

For people with severe hypoglycemia, large quantities of carbo-hydrates can be highly detrimental. Hypoglycemics, who require triple the protein of the average person, should emphasize protein storage.

Nutritional balance. Fats are an essential part of the diet. Olive oil is preferable to other shortenings because it has more nutritional value. It will keep for several years when stored in a cool, dark place. Metal containers are preferable to glass for long-term storage. But when push comes to shove, lard is an adequate source of fat.

The amount and type of food a person needs depends on many things: the level of activity (the higher the intensity, the more food will be needed); age (a teenager burns food more quickly than an adult); height and weight; and weather conditions. Generally, a person working out of doors will need between 2,500 and 3,500 calories per day.

Emergency food rations. "Cookie" bars that have been specially formulated for high protein, vitamin, and mineral content are Coast Guard–approved and are available at NitroPak (see the section on products and services on page 161). This is the only place I have seen them. Other food bars are available in stores everywhere in flavors to suit every taste. However, some ingredients such as corn syrup, sugar, and barley malt may not be suitable for everyone. If you have found a food bar that works for you, lay in a supply in an airtight container or two.

Textured vegetable protein (TVP) is a soy product that is free of gluten, sugar, dairy, and animal products. Soy is said to be an excellent source of protein and calcium, but exclusive use of TVP may not be appropriate for those who require animal protein. That said, TVP is a tasty alternative food that should be in everyone's larder as backup, if nothing else. Many TVP products can be stored for extended periods. These products are certified kosher and can be obtained by catalog or on-line. (See page 157 for information.)

MREs, or meals-ready-to-eat, were developed by the military. Unlike their predecessors, the military C-rations and K-rations of World War II, they are varied and tasty. As the name indicates, MREs can be eaten anywhere, any time, hot or cold. They require no preparation.

Camping pouch products, such as Alpine Aire's Ready Reserve Foods and Mountain House, are meals in a pouch—literally. You add boiling water, wait ten minutes and eat, right out of the pouch or not. Selections are interesting, as for example Mountain House Beef Teriyaki, which is quite tasty. They can be found in sporting goods and camping stores.

If you are taking supplements such as multiple vitamins, minerals, herbals, and essential oils, be sure to stock an adequate supply in airtight containers in a cool, dry place. Note the expiration dates on the bottles or boxes, using first those that expire earliest.

If you are not taking supplements at this time, consider doing so. In an emergency, fresh, nutritious foods may not be readily available, and stored food loses nutritional value over time. In any case, under conditions of stress, your system will need all the support you can give it, especially Vitamin C.

CHAPTER 16

Clothing and Bedding

We have had a run of very mild winters in recent years, and if we're lucky, the winter of 1999–2000 will be one of them. But it's not something we can count on. When the weather is extremely cold, heating supplies are used up more rapidly than normal. If, in addition to severe weather, there are power outages, the resulting "deep freeze" can be a threat to health and safety.

Housing in warmer parts of the country often lack heating systems, so cold spells, when they come, are hard on people—especially the aged and infirm. It's a good idea to lay in a supply of sweaters, blankets, and, yes, sleeping bags.

Warm clothing is the simple, practical response to cold. Layered clothing holds air, which has the effect of trapping your body heat, so have several sweaters of various weights to put on or take off as needed. Even if you've never done so before, consider buying long underwear. It's hard to beat for effectiveness. Wool socks are another surefire warmer. If one pair doesn't do the job, wear two.

Hats and caps are important—you lose a great deal of your body heat through your head. You can wear a hat around the house and to bed, too, if it's cold enough.

Avoid going out in rain, sleet, snow, or high winds. Also avoid exertion that causes you to sweat. The important thing is to stay dry because no clothing can be warm if it is wet. A waterproof poncho might be used over a warm coat. Beware cheap plastic, as it becomes brittle and will crack and leak in extreme cold. Be sure warm, sturdy boots are a part of the preparations.

Warmth at night. Have two or three extra blankets per person. Wool is tough and warm, but some synthetics are lighter, more durable, and don't retain moisture. Sleeping bags are an excellent way to manage icy conditions. A sleeping bag, which slides nicely into your bed, will give you a comfortable night even if it's really frigid.

Good sleeping bags carry ratings for degrees of temperature they will withstand. Try a camping store or outfitter's catalogue such as L. L. Bean for help in selecting an appropriate type of sleeping bag.

Consider purchasing a few inflatable mattresses. If, for example, you have heat in your house and members of your family or friends do not, you may find yourself with unexpected company. Inflatables will make your guests a little more comfortable. (By the way, you can conserve heat by closing off rooms that you don't need.)

Hypothermia can kill. In our usually well-heated world, where cars, buses, and trains take us from one point to the other in comfort and safety, we seldom think of cold as an actual health hazard. But hypothermia, a life-threatening condition, occurs when the core temperature of your torso—which is normally at a constant 98.6°F—drops to between 95°F and 77°F. Avoid anything that can cause abrupt, uncontrolled loss of body heat.

Symptoms of hypothermia include loss of coordination, sluggishness, and impaired judgment. To treat hypothermia, consult a first-aid book; if possible, get the victim to a hospital.

Don't discard any clothing, shoes, or blankets; others may be very happy to have what you no longer need. Call local charities such as the Salvation Army for a pickup or for the address where you can drop off donations. Ask your local volunteer fire departments and/or rescue squads if they are set up to accept such donations.

CHAPTER 17

Home Sanitation

It comes as an unpleasant surprise to the uninitiated that when the power goes out, in time, so does the plumbing. That's because in most cases water pressure is maintained by electrical pumps and computerized servo-mechanisms.

You may find you have nonfunctioning toilets. If you have a pond nearby or rainbarrels or some other source of unfiltered water, you can flush your toilet that way. Otherwise, here's where a huge supply of large plastic garbage bags comes in handy. The toilet bowl will be empty of water; line it with a garbage bag. After every use, scatter a quarter cup of lime (available at any garden store) or borax over the waste. This should help to keep down the odors.

People who have wood stoves should keep the ashes, as they are also effective in masking odors. Bags should be replaced at least daily, depending on the usage.

There will be those who can dig a latrine some distance away from the house. If this is possible (the frozen ground makes for tough digging), follow the same routine after use by sprinkling the latrine pit with lime or borax.

Without water to wash hands and dishes, soil builds up, increasing exposure to germs. Cans of disinfectant such as Lysol should be put in the kitchen, as well as in the bathroom. Use isopropyl alcohol to clean keyboards and telephones (if they're working). A new hand cleanser called *Purell* works without water. It comes in large and small dispensers; the latter do well in purses or back pockets.

If you find naptha soap, buy a supply. It's a disinfectant and works wonderfully well in the laundry.

Using paper products, such as plates, cups, and bowls should cut down on water usage, but it will add to the waste-disposal burden. Burning paper and other trash is hazardous and should not be attempted unless you are equipped to do so. (Agricultural Districts routinely allow for burning.)

Garbage pickup may not be working, so the bags should be stored in a secure area, away from food storage, until such time as it can safely be disposed of. Double bag *all* waste. Store waste either outside in the frozen weather or inside somewhere that vermin, animals, and children can't get to it.

Human waste requires special disposal. Burial is preferable, even though, again, there's the problem of the ground being frozen. It should never be mixed with your regular composting material. Try to generate as little waste as possible. This is a sound idea regardless of Y2K problems.

CHAPTER 18

Prescriptions and Preparing for Medical Emergencies

The medical profession does not seem to be any more aware of the Y2K problem than the rest of the world. Nevertheless, it's important for you to get your doctor to focus on the possibility of an interruption in the delivery of medical supplies. Remind him or her that some of these medications come from overseas and that there probably will be some delivery problems. If you are using insulin or some other vitally important medication, ask your physician if you can have (and fill) prescriptions well in advance. All of this is better addressed now than later.

Preserving medications. If your medication requires refrigeration, you must figure out now how you will protect it. Hopefully, your municipal authority will plan for the central storage of perishable pharmaceutical items.

Avoid medical emergencies. If you know that you need elective surgery, get it done now. You don't want to have an emergency just when the whole medical delivery system is under stress. The same applies to dentistry. If you think everything is OK, don't just hope—get yourself and your family to the dentist for a checkup. Also be sure to get to the eye doctor and have an extra pair of prescription eyeglasses made up.

If you have a serious medical condition, and do not already have Medic Alert, now would be a good time to enroll. You will receive either a bracelet or medallion (to hang around your neck like a dog tag) with information as to your allergies, your blood type, and so forth. Medic Alert can be reached at 1–800–633–4260.

Do you need any boosters? When is the last time you had a tetanus shot? Or a polio shot? Are there any preventive injections your doctor recommends, such as the kind one has when traveling to an undeveloped country? If there are extended water emergencies in your area because of Y2K, conditions could become very primitive very rapidly.

If your doctor is located nearby, you are fortunate. But be sure to ask where he or she plans to be when Y2K arrives. If it's out of town or he or she plans to retire, find another physician at once and—very important—find one near where you live.

Consider taking a first-aid course. The Red Cross and many community organizations offer basic first aid classes. Learn cardio-pulmonary resuscitation (CPR) and also the Heimlich maneuver, a technique to help someone who is choking. Your local emergency medical training (EMT) may offer training.

PART III

Money Matters and Y2K

Telling people to have money on hand is easier said than done. However, if everyone in the family concentrates on the project, you will probably be able to amass a fair amount—just in case the checks don't arrive in the mail or your credit cards or your ATMs aren't working.

CHAPTER 19

Have Cash on Hand

The banking system as a whole is further along in fixing the Y2K problem than any other sector of the economy. Still there are likely to be many glitches and systems failures, and some individual banks are seriously lagging. Therefore, you need to know the Y2K status of any bank in which you have deposits, CDs, savings/ retirement accounts, and such. It's important to check not just the branch you use, but the entire corporation.

ATMs are entirely automated, so if anything in the bank fails, they probably will. It would be a good idea to start stockpiling cash. Take a little more out each time than you normally do, and set it aside. This takes discipline, but you may be very glad you took this step.

Asking questions at your bank isn't enough. You should put your questions in writing. Send your letter to your branch bank by certified mail, return receipt requested. If the answer is only vaguely reassuring, with no specifics other than "we will be compliant in time," consider transferring to another bank. (A sample letter to your bank can be found on page 95.)

Prepare for an interruption in bank services. Plan to set aside enough money for a two-to-eight-week period. Currency should be in used bills, in denominations of twenty dollars or less. Also rolls of quarters may very well come in handy.

Gold and silver may be acquired as a backup. Coins are sometimes more useful than paper money. Small-denomination bullion would probably be best—not coins that have numismatic value, since they are not likely to fetch what they are worth. Canadian Maple Leaves or Krugerrands of varying weights can be purchased from local coin dealers or by mail. Always compare prices—including taxes and shipping—before making a buy.

Pre-1965 US coins have silver content. Bags of these coins, called "junk silver," are available from the same dealers.

CHAPTER 20

The Check's in the Mail

While the Social Security Administration (SSA) has been working on Y2K remediation since 1991, having first identified the problem in 1989, they are not finished seven years later, in 1998. Of all federal agencies, they are furthest along, and there are many reasons to hope that they will make the deadline.

Social Security is just the start. SSA does not issue checks. Instead, SSA sends notification of the amounts of the pension or other entitlement checks to the Treasury Department's Financial Management System (FMS). It, in turn, electronically transfers the funds to designated banks. As of January 1, 1999, all such checks will be totally automated, and paper checks will be discontinued.

There are weak links in this chain. As of this writing, the Treasury Department is far behind in its remediation. In a midyear review of the situation, Congressman Stephen Horn, Chairman of the House Subcommittee on Y2K, gave Treasury a grade of D. Other areas of weakness are the banking system (even though they are further along than everyone else) and telecommunications companies. No enterprise in this chain of linked computer systems is yet Y2K-compliant.

What about private pension funds? If you have money in a corporate or government retirement fund, the question of whether your checks will go out on time is, again, a Y2K issue. It might be a good idea to ask the managers of your pension funds how far along they are in Y2K remediation and whether they have checked on their electronic links to banks. Are they studying the Y2K vulnerabilities of each of their stock holdings? You can write to your pension-fund manager just as you would your bank. (See page 95.)

CHAPTER 21

You and Your Job

According to one source, as of May 1, 1998, 40 percent of major corporations had not finished even a survey of the their Y2K status. This means they have not actually begun to work on the problem. According to another survey, only 30 percent have done the basic work. A sobering fact about any disruption of business is that some fragile or marginal companies are likely to fail. If there is long-term disruption from Y2K, your job may be in jeopardy.

Do you know how your company is doing? Finding this out is the first step in evaluating your own prospects.

Get your résumé ready. This is always a good idea because it helps you to think clearly about the present and the future of your job. And, if you will have to go job-hunting, it's good to have your résumé, at the ready.

Maybe you really don't want to keep your present job or any job like it. The recent wholesale downsizing by business and industry has produced many casualties, but in hindsight it wasn't all bad for everyone. Some workers eventually got jobs elsewhere similar to the ones they had lost—some did better, some did worse. But we keep hearing about people who picked up, moved away, and started their own businesses. Success comes in many forms, which is something to bear in mind if you lose your job because of Y2K.

If you own a small business, you might think about streamlining your operations. Computer expert and consultant Ed Yourdon suggests turning off any non-mission-critical systems now. If yours is a just-in-time inventory system, you might consider some contingency stockpiling.

It's a good idea to ask your vendors and suppliers pointed questions about their status—have they started Y2K remediation, how much code do they have, how much have they budgeted for repairs, how many people are working on the project, and so on. If you are not satisfied with the their responses, consider lining up other vendors and suppliers.

CHAPTER 22

Going Back to Barter

B arter is an ancient form of commerce. You give something, you get something in return. But in our culture, at this late hour of the twentieth century bartering is an almost alien practice. We are accustomed to the availability of an abundance of merchandise at fixed prices. We are also accustomed to paying by cash, check, and credit cards. The idea of swapping one thing for something entirely different—say a gallon of water for a box of matches—calls for a major shift in the way we think.

The return of barter? Barter could become important if you and your family were isolated by snow, power outages, or some other condition. Or if, because of power outages, your ATM or your credit cards weren't working, it might be very convenient to have some things on hand to trade for necessities. (Below is a list of items that have in the past been good as "currency"—that is, easily portable, durable, divisible goods of obvious worth.) Remember that you can barter your labor, such as chopping wood, in exchange for things you need. An able body is an asset not to be overlooked.

There are perils to bartering. In times of shortage, you run the risk of being robbed. So it's best if you barter only with people you know or in a swap meet or a farmers-market type of setting. Don't talk to strangers about what you have to barter or where you live (presumably, where your barterables are stored).

Think about what to do in an emergency. Obviously, there are people you can and should help—the elderly, infirm, children, and so forth. They are the reason for stockpiling more than just enough for yourselves. But you are likely to be approached by other, able-bodied people who are unprepared to take care of themselves and will expect others (you) simply to supply them with what they need. You will have to use your head to determine how or whether to turn them down. Or, if they are insistent, what work you will ask of them in return for some barterable item.

Useful barter items. These items are routinely found on barter lists. You can add whatever else you feel is appropriate:

Alcohol—the drinking kind, including wines. Preferably in small bottles, pints, half pints, and the one-drink size that are sold on planes

Ammunition—primarily .22 shells and buckshot

Aspirin/acetaminophen

Candles

Canning jars and lids

Chlorine bleach, in liquid form

Chocolate—solid kind, candy bars, kisses (store in airtight containers)

Cigarettes—any brand (Some people are so strongly opposed to tobacco that this would be offensive—however, cigarette packs and cartons have been popular since World War II, when they were a staple of the black market in Europe.)

Cigars

Cocoa—sweetened and unsweetened

Coffee—beans in airtight containers

Condiments—mustard, ketchup, mayonnaise, soy, BBQ sauce (in individual packets)

Food—canned goods

Kerosene

Light bulbs (for when the lights come back on)

Lighters—the disposable kind

Lime—large sacks (used to deodorize waste and accelerate the rate of decay)

Motor oil

Pencils and paper

Pet food

Powdered drink mixes such as Kool-Aid

Sanitary supplies—toilet paper, feminine products, trash bags, bars of soap

Seeds—nonhybrid/open pollinating

Shortening

Silver—pre-1965 U.S. coins

Soda—in cans

Teabags

Wine

CHAPTER 23

Get Paper Copies of Important Documents

If there is a disruption of electronic services, you should have a hard copy (that is to say, a paper copy) of important documents. Without an official hard copy of the document, you may not be able to prove some things you need to prove—such as your age, citizenship, marital status, property ownership, debts owed and paid, and so on.

Where should you store your records? The answer used to be automatic: in your safe-deposit box at the bank. However, in a national emergency the government could declare a bank holiday (as President Franklin D. Roosevelt did in 1933). You might be denied access to your safe-deposit box for some time. Therefore, to be sure you can get your hands on your data when you need it, keep paper copies in a small, fireproof home safe. These safes are available in stationary stores and superstores such as Sears and Staples. If possible, make a duplicate set and put the extra set in your safe-deposit box at the bank. These are kinds of documents to safeguard:

1. Birth certificate for every member of the family
2. Naturalization papers
3. Death certificates
4. Marriage licenses and certificates
5. Divorce records
6. Baptismal, confirmation, ordination, and other religious records
7. Name change affidavits
8. Social Security cards (To get Personal Earnings and Benefit Estimate Statements from the Social Security Administration, call their national toll-free number (1–800–772–1213) and ask for a copy of form SSA–7004. Easier yet, fill out a copy on the SSA's web site at www.ssa.gov. You can also get this form from your local SSA office. Complete the form and mail it in. You should get a recent copy of your statement in the mail in about six weeks.)
9. Insurance policies, including life, home, tenants', credit card, car, boat, and so forth
10. Voter-registration card
11. Deeds, titles, plot maps, surveys, and other proofs of ownership
12. Mortgages and other loan agreements
13. Property tax records
14. Planning and zoning records
15. Inspections and permits
16. Business licenses
17. Incorporation records
18. Court proceedings, including judgments and liens, civil cases, criminal cases, adoption records, juvenile records
19. Selective Service information

20. Automobile, boat, and airplane registration records
21. Drivers' licenses
22. Hunting and fishing licenses
23. Tax returns for the past five years
24. Parents should be able to procure records of children's immunizations (tetanus, polio, chicken pox, etc.) from the school nurse or from their family physician.

We can expect billing glitches. These can come from just about anywhere. To forestall the problem if any of your suppliers or creditors should bill you incorrectly, have at least the last three months of statements from 1999, plus current canceled checks, for the following: rent, mortgage, common charges, electricity, gas, telephone, water and credit cards.

Erratic computers might dredge up charges that you have already paid. So keep on hand copies of any kind of dispute— claims, overcharges, and such—and particularly correspondence showing that the problem was resolved.

PART IV

Life Goes on Regardless of Y2K

"If you were marooned on a desert island, what books would you want to have with you?" Consider this an update of that old question. For a time, at least, you and your family may be thrown on your own resources. So long as you are physically all right, this may not be a bad thing.

CHAPTER 24

Your Home Computer, Mac or PC

It comes as a shock to many to learn that the Y2K issue is not limited to mainframe computers—it affects desktops and laptops as well. Here's an overview of what you'll need to do:

Macintoshes don't have a hardware problem, because they were built with internal timing components that use four-digit fields. However, Mac software applications may have the same kind of issues as PCs, and will need to be reviewed.

First, look at the PC computer platform itself. Because such elements as the basic input/output systems (BIOS) and the real time clock (RTC) are the traffic cops for date usage in PCs, they must be Y2K-compliant to function. (Test samples of a wide variety of PCs manufactured before 1997 showed that up to 93 percent of them had BIOS and/or RTC problems.) Get the manufacturer's model and serial number off your PC, and then visit the company's Web site to see if anything has been posted about the Y2K status of your model. Don't rely on verbal assurances from a tech support hotline. Write the manufacturer and ask for a reply in writing. For an excellent overview on Y2K and PCs, visit the Web site of Mitre Corporation (www.mitre.org/research /cots/compliant-BIOS.htm).

Some operating systems, including DOS and pre-Windows 95, have Y2K problems. For these and other Microsoft applications, visit their product-guide Web page (www.microsoft.com /ithome/topics/year2k/product/product.htm) to determine the Y2K status of your operating system.

Commercial Off-the-Shelf (COTS) software applications should be checked. Make a list of each application you have purchased and contact the vendor to determine compliance and the current or projected availability and cost of Y2K upgrades.

Your own data files need to be reviewed, even if your PC, operating system, and software applications are Y2K compliant. The issue is how you have entered data in your spreadsheets and databases. If any date comparisons or calculations are being used and you have only entered two digits for the year, you will probably have to correct your past entries if you plan to use the data in 2000.

Caution: **You risk corrupting your system** if you attempt to reset dates on a PC. Don't act until you are clear about what you are doing.

CHAPTER 25

Personal Communication During an Emergency

No one can know if radio and TV transmissions will go down or become erratic, but it is well to assume that they might. To get the news—and possibly civil defense instructions from your local government—keep a battery-operated radio on hand.

Equipment that doesn't depend on electricity includes battery-operated shortwave radios such as those made by Sangean. Then there is the wind-up BayGen Freeplay Radio AM/FM that doesn't use batteries and has a solar-powered option.

For one-mile-radius communication (or less), there are Motorola Talkabout two-way radios. These are small, technically advanced, battery-operated walkie-talkies.

Citizen-band (CB) radios, which are widely used by truckers, can send and receive messages. If you and one or two of your neighbors have CBs and the batteries or generators to sustain their use, you have the makings of a support network. Two manufacturers produce exceptional products: Uniden (especially their economical PC–122XL) and Cobra (with its top-of-the-line 2010GTLWX base CB transceiver.)

Ham-radio operators have been lifesavers in the past, and it is to be hoped that they will be able to function well in the future. However, if Y2K outcomes are severe, the repeater networks that hams rely on may well be in jeopardy. If you are not now a ham operator and want to consider this option, more power to you, so to speak.

CHAPTER 26

Getting Around—Public and Personal Transportation

Almost every form of transportation has been computerized—trains, planes, buses, river traffic on inland waterways—you name it. The bigger the system, the more likely it is to be computer-dependent. Most of these systems run on fuels that are supplied by pipelines, and pipelines, in turn, are entirely computerized. So some outages seem likely.

Cars have been called computers on wheels. But the extent to which they are in jeopardy from computer error is simply not known. When my wife took our four-month-old UTE in for service, she was told that the "EVO" had "a bad chip" and that it would have to be replaced. Diagnostics are performed with a computerized, hand-held tool. Whenever any repairs or upgrades are required, the manufacturer simply sends a disk that is uploaded into the unit. This in turn attaches to the vehicle and updates that system. A far cry from the grease-monkey days.

Carpools are excellent because they conserve fuel. They also help to build personal relationships for mutual support. However, it is important to know in advance if any gas stations in your area have generators to supply the power necessary to pump gas if the electricity fails.

An interesting question for your local police is what rules will apply if the traffic lights fail. It's unlikely that the police will have the personnel to direct traffic. A solution should be found well in advance.

When you travel in times of emergency, let others know where you are going, by what route, and when you expect to arrive. It's best if you can travel with a companion. Travel during daylight hours, and pay attention to weather information. If a storm is predicted, wait until it clears; braving bad weather may be a bad decision.

If you are stranded, stay with your car. Run the motor for short periods to get warmth from the heater, but always keep a window opened a crack for fresh air. Use a flashlight to read or signal for help rather than the headlights—you want to conserve battery power. See the checklist on page 131 for supplies you should consider carrying in your car.

In a dire emergency, you can get insulation for your body by cutting foam from your car seats. Foam padding is a wonderful insulator. Put it next to your skin and wrap your feet in it. You can always repair the car seat.

Bicycles are a fine alternative means of transportation for your immediate area. They are relatively cheap (compared to cars), convenient, and good exercise. It's also a good idea to travel in groups. In snowy suburban and rural areas, consider winter hiking boots, snowshoes, and cross-country skis.

CHAPTER 27

"Meanwhile, Back at the Ranch . . ."

If we assume a fairly severe disruption in services, because of a combination of Y2K and bad weather, you and your family will probably be confronted with a strange new pattern of life. And you'll probably be seeing a lot more of one another than you do in the course of an ordinary week. Here are a few things to think about:

It's not forever. Having to conserve water and use candles instead of electricity is inconvenient, but it's not fatal. It would be natural for children to be very upset (particularly if their schools close either because they can't function or because they have been taken over as temporary shelters). And teenagers may balk at the confinement. These responses must be dealt with firmly for everyone's sake.

Everyone should have appropriate tasks, depending on the person's age and skills. This is not a time to expect Mom or Dad to do everything. Teaching homemaking and home-maintenance skills to the kids should be part of your emergency plan.

Build as much structure and routine as possible. A systematic "spring cleaning" of the house, involving every family member would have real merit. In the fall of 1999, have a conference with your children's teachers to set up a program to follow in the event of a temporary but prolonged school closing. Then have brief classes every day to be sure your children keep up.

In the absence of TV, and with computer games off limits because they use up batteries, be sure to have books, magazines, and games on hand. This is a good time to rediscover the art of conversation and perhaps to discuss what everyone thinks about this strange disruption of our lives.

Write a family log or diary. You can record everything from an inventory of supplies to personal feelings.

In the case of a single person going through a Y2K dislocation by him- or herself, it's possible to feel very isolated and depressed. The key to good morale is keeping in touch with relatives, friends, and neighbors. Better still, it's a good idea to get out and help others who need assistance.

Getting together with neighbors is another way of keeping in touch and lightening the atmosphere. And it's a fine old frontier tradition.

For those with religious convictions, this is prime time for contemplation and prayer. Be sure to have a copy of the Bible and other devotional books on hand. The events leading up to Y2K can most certainly be reviewed and examined for the spiritual lessons that can be drawn from them.

PART V

Y2K and the Public Sector

Americans have a genius for organizing themselves. All we really need is information about the problems we are facing. Once this is available, we can not only provide for ourselves, but we can also care for those in need of help—the young, the aged, and the infirm.

CHAPTER 28

Is Your Local Government Ready for Emergencies?

Your ability to find out what is going on in your community and city depends largely on where you live. Two-thirds of Americans live in metropolitan areas that contain at least one city of at least fifty thousand people. Typically, governments in such areas are fragmented into counties, municipalities, school districts, and special-purpose districts (such as airports, utilities, mass transit, sanitation, and public-housing districts).

The result of municipal fragmentation is uncoordinated service, competition for financial resources, and duplication of facilities. Y2K presents an enormous challenge to people in such urban areas. Merely finding out who does what can be a life work.

You need answers to basic questions about how 911 will function if automated systems fail. Ask whether the police, fire, and medical emergency systems have been checked and tested for Y2K compliance. What contingency plans does the city have to deal with power outages, failure of the water supply, sewage treatment, and hospital and health maintenance? What about methadone clinics? Such services cannot be abruptly terminated without dire consequences—people whose addictions are under control would be thrown into severe stress.

What about outright civil disorder? What plans have been made to control large-scale demonstrations or disorder? If, for example, looting starts, who will be there to stop it? Will the city be able to call on adjacent jurisdictions? Have they made commitments to aid others?

Start at the top. Identify the key decision makers, the mayor or city manager, the president of the city council, the chief of police, and so on. Your purpose is to get elected officials and senior managers to realize that questions of public welfare must be addressed. Government-sponsored meetings are notoriously underattended. You should start attending yours and asking questions there.

There is strength in numbers. An individual acting alone cannot deal with the fallout from the failure of automated systems. But Americans have a talent for organizing and enlisting help in order to accomplish specific missions. In every community there is a network of businesses, homeowners associations, service organizations, fraternal orders, and religious organizations. They are a good place to start. Also consult the Chamber of Commerce, real estate boards, the Jaycees, Rotary, Kiwanis, Lions, Soroptimists, Elks, Masons, and so forth. Contact their leaders and find out if they have plans to handle any aspect of crisis management. For example, do they have plans in place to care for the elderly and disabled who cannot take care of themselves?

If you have a special concern, such as the need for dialysis or some other service crucially dependent on electricity, you will need specific reassurances. Priests, ministers, rabbis, and heads of local organizations who are used to dealing with local government and community issues may be able to help "show you the ropes" in getting through to the right people in the bureaucracies.

Local businesses are part of the picture. They can be an important source of help in this crisis, so contact them and discuss what they can contribute to emergency planning. Also discuss how to ensure their continued functioning, because they, too, will need protection from civil disorder.

In his book *Going Local*, Michael H. Shuman makes the point that we cannot afford to lose factories, offices, shops, or farms. "Those enterprises are the lifeblood of the community. They provide the jobs that keep families alive. They pump up the local economy through sales, savings, and investment. They pay the income, property, and sales taxes that finance schools, hospitals, police, and street repairs."

CHAPTER 29

Public Health Issues

We give little thought to the urban systems that ensure our public health—drinkable water, sewage treatment, garbage disposal, and hospitals and clinics. Most of these systems are dependent on electricity. If power fails for any length of time, these systems will be at risk.

Water and sewage systems installed in the 1950s or earlier are not likely to have serious Y2K problems, the more modern systems, which have many automated functions, are highly vulnerable. Pumping, chemical treatment, flow regulation, metering, and billing are now in the realm of the computer—a sort of no-man's land, where computers really run things and where few skilled people stand ready to take over in an emergency.

Hospitals are also computer dependent. Miraculous advances in medical technology are almost all wedded to the computer. MRIs, blood analysis, dialysis, you name it. Like municipal water systems, many hospitals have backup generators. Stockpiled fuel will be an important consideration for them. A two-week stockpile of fuel would seem to be adequate. But the Northeast power blackout during the winter of 1997–1998 lasted four to six weeks (depending on location). So it would seem prudent to adjust stockpile estimates upward.

So effective is modern sanitation that few people in industrialized nations ever worry about epidemics. But as people who have lived through floods and hurricanes can attest, sanitary systems are vulnerable. Consider getting the kind of shots you would need if you were traveling in an undeveloped country. Ask your doctor or local health department for guidance.

CHAPTER 30

A Momentous New Year's Eve

In contrast to the turn of the last millennium in A.D. 999—with its local plagues, famines, and invading Vikings, Moors, and Magyars—ours is a scientific age that encompasses the whole globe. The functioning of minuscule chips and ephemeral lines of software will determine whether we pass this milestone with or without a jolt.

The second millennium will come first to New Zealand and will work its way to Australia, Asia, the Middle East, Europe, Africa, Latin America, North America, and, finally, Hawaii.

This is one New Year's Eve when you won't want to go to bed early. In the United States, we will be receiving reports from the advancing front, word of how the world fares, hour by hour. Will there be breakdown of automated systems or not?

About thirty to sixty minutes before midnight, you should consider protecting your major electrical appliances, such as refrigerators and computers, from possible power surges by unplugging them. If the power is still on by 2:00 A.M., you can consider plugging them back in.

If you have been persuaded to make some preparations, you will be ready with candles, flashlights, a supply of food, and other essentials. And you will have thought through responses to any short- or long-term failures in the heating system in your house, and any other such problems.

We can all hope that the critical infrastructure—electricity, gas, water, telecommunications, transportation, and banking—will not fail. We can hope that the turbulence will be spotty and brief, and that there will be unaffected areas that will be able to come to the aid of those that are.

But for the sake of all—ourselves, our families and friends, our communities, and our nation—it is now clear that prudent preparations should be made at every level to preserve civil order and our quality of life. The sections that follow offer sample letters to your representatives and specifics on checklists, products and sources, and references.

PART VI

Political Action

Let's tell our government representatives that we want a realistic evaluation of the situation. Senator Daniel Patrick Moynihan, in a letter to the President on July 31, 1996, said that there is "the question of whether there is enough time to get the job done and, if not, what sort of triage we may need." Okay, what *are* our priorities?

CHAPTER 31

What Should You Ask Your State Legislators?

Anyone now holding or planning to hold elective office had better bone up on Y2K issues immediately because the electorate is going to be asking some very pointed questions. Here are a few you may want to send by mail, fax, or E-mail to your own state representatives:

1. **As legislators, leaders, chairs of committees,** can you say that the government programs you oversee are on schedule for timely Y2K compliance?

2. **State regulatory commissions** with oversight of utilities, insurance, banking, and so on should rigorously pursue fact-finding. What is the true situation in each of these industries?

3. **Have criteria been developed** for measuring progress? How often are your departments reporting to you?

4. **Have emergency-response networks** (including 911, police, fire, and emergency medical services) from state to local levels been directed to add Y2K scenarios to their disaster-recovery plans?

5. **What level of staffing does the state have** to deal with Y2K issues? How many people? Is there an outreach program to be sure that counties, cities, schools, and special districts receive guidance? Is there a means to build awareness, share success stories, and urge action?

6. **How will skilled programmers be retained?** Are state pay scales competitive with those of industry? Bearing in mind that the loss of skilled labor can cripple government remediation efforts, what is being done? Are retention bonuses being considered?

7. **Is anyone watching the state's purse strings?** Controls will be needed to make sure that everyone has a firm hold on the first priority—which is to bring existing equipment into compliance. Of course, there are situations where it will be more efficient to get new equipment than to try to fix the old. Has someone been appointed to ensure that the Y2K crisis doesn't become an excuse for lavish spending?

8. **Insist that the political parties work together.** This is an important point to be stressed in any correspondence with officials and or party leaders. This is no time for one party to score points off the other.

CHAPTER 32

To Whom Should You Write?

You should share your concerns with your elected representatives on the federal, state, and local levels. Urge them to investigate the Y2K status of vital services and apply pressure—and funding—to make sure that everything possible will be done to prevent Y2K breakdowns. However late it may be, there are still things that can and should be done.

Addresses. In this age of faxes and E-mail, you may want to communicate electronically. If you choose to write, letters—and postcards—are still very effective ways to get your message across.

To get the names of your representatives, phone the local office of your party or the League of Women Voters. Here are the three key federal addresses:

President Bill Clinton
The White House
Washington, DC 20500

[Your senator's name]
The Senate of the United States
Washington, DC 20500

[Your representative's name]
The House of Representatives
Washington, DC 20515

Ask for the state and local names and addresses of your representatives at the same time you call about your senators and members of Congress. People who have information about one group usually know all the key players.

If you have particular concerns, such as how the government is going to handle the airport traffic near you, you may want to go directly to the chairs of the congressional or legislative oversight committees. This information can be found in almanacs.

On the local level, perhaps you are concerned about the feeding of the indigent in a crisis. In New York City alone, 800,000 people are dependent on the city and charities for food. This is not something that can be left to chance. And will drug maintenance programs continue? This is not the setting in which desperate people should be asked to go "cold turkey."

Write on only one subject. Don't piggyback other topics on the main one—it causes problems for the people who process the mail. Keep your message clear, simple, and *civil*.

CHAPTER 33

Sample Letters

I f you are worried about what will happen to computer records during the Y2K changeover to the year 2000, it makes sense for you to write to your local bank and ask specific questions. This is a letter that is worth sending Certified Mail: Return Receipt Requested. Then keep the reply with your other banking papers.

A sample letter to your bank:

[Date]
[Title]
[Department]
[Street]
[City, State, Zip]

Dear [ ]:

As a customer of your bank, I am greatly concerned about the year-2000 problem and its possible impact on my account [checking account #00000000 and/or savings account #000000]. Specifically, I would like to ask these questions:

1. What assurances can you give that [name of the institution] will be able to provide timely and accurate service in the event of power, communication, and/or equipment failure?
2. Will ATMs and debit cards function?
3. Will customer records and accounts continue to reflect activity regardless of Y2K interruptions?
4. Does the bank have hard-copy backup for each account?

I would appreciate a written response to my questions as soon as possible. Please do not send a generic form letter saying everything's fine. I need to know specifics.

Sincerely,
[Name]
[Address]
[City, State, Zip]
[Phone]

A sample letter to your representative:

[Same heading as above]

Dear [elected official]:

I am deeply concerned about the year-2000 computer problem. I want to know what you are doing personally to ensure that this potential disaster will be minimized as much as time and resources allow.

I trust that we agree that this isn't simply a computer issue, but a threat to our economy, public safety, and quality of life.

In electing you, we trusted that you would present our concerns to your colleagues and the nation and that you would do everything in your power to secure our general welfare by dealing forcefully with such issues.

Please let me know your evaluation of Y2K and what you have proposed or done about it.

Sincerely,
[Same closing as above]

Postcards are another good way to get your message to your elected representatives. Keep your message short—don't cram more onto the card than can easily be read. Make it your best penmanship. And put your name and address on it, if you want a reply.

Dear [elected official]:
I want to know if our federal surplus is being used to deal with the Y2K problem. Please reply.

Sincerely,
[Name]
[Address]
[City, State, Zip]
[Phone]

PART VII

Master Checklists

The purpose of these lists is to help you to focus on what you should consider storing up. You probably already have on hand most of what you'll need. Certainly no one needs all of these things.

Directory to Checklists

Your financial resources and storage facilities have limits, so look at the appropriate lists with an eye to the highest priorities. And, of course, you already have a great many of the items mentioned. Use the margins on these checklist pages for notes, and consult others for their advice. The choices you make are your responsibility.

Before you throw up your hands in despair, think about the specifics of your situation. How many people are in your household? Will anyone be coming to stay with you? If so, add to your supplies. (Another person in the household can help with responsibilities, going on errands, helping to corral the children, and so forth.) Don't forget the needs of your pets.

Many survival checklists are available. Family needs vary greatly. Some will need pet supplies or supplies for unique medical conditions. So review our lists, delete what doesn't apply, and add what you will need.

The checklists are organized as follows:

1

Organizing Supplies

To setup emergency housekeeping either in the home or elsewhere, consider assembling the following:

☐ cash in coins (for example, rolls of quarters) and currency (twenty-dollar bills are preferable to higher denominations; checks and credit cards may not function in times of emergency)

☐ food and water (see page 113)

☐ cooking equipment (see page 108)

☐ source of light—candles, battery-operated Coleman lanterns

☐ battery-operated or solar-charged radio

☐ clock, the wind-up, alarm variety

☐ fire extinguisher

☐ whistles for communication (everyone should have one to hang around the neck or carry in a pocket)

- ☐ manual, solar-powered, or battery-operated calculator

- ☐ paper—ruled and unruled pads

- ☐ pencils, pens, crayons

- ☐ envelopes and stamps (although mail service will probably be disrupted for a time on a regional basis)

- ☐ calendar

- ☐ address books

- ☐ maps of your region

- ☐ typewriter (nonelectric), extra ribbons, typewriter paper

- ☐ toys for children

- ☐ cards, puzzles, games

- ☐ bicycles (ideally, one for each member of the family or group), tire repair kits, manual air pump

- ☐ first-aid kit (see page 118 for specifics)

- ☐ important documents in a fireproof carrying case (see page 65 for this checklist)

2

Basic Food Supplies

We use the recommendation of the Church of Latter Day Saints as our standard for food storage, given their experience in this area. The rule is store what you eat and eat what you store. That said, it's helpful to know how much food is necessary to keep on hand. The recommended amounts for *a three-month period* for one person age twelve or older are given below.

Basic food items and amounts. Scale this up or down as you feel appropriate (some people prefer to increase legumes up to 150 pounds and reduce the amount of grains accordingly). You'll need to add fruits, vegetables, and vitamins and mineral supplements, as needed.

☐ grains: 105 lbs.—wheat, enriched white flour, spelt, amaranth, kamut, cornmeal, rolled oats, rice, pearled barley, spaghetti, and macaroni

☐ legumes: 10 lbs.—beans, lima, soy, split peas, lentils, drysoup mix

☐ fats and oils: 7 lbs.—vegetable oil, olive oil, shortening, mayonnaise, nut butters

- [ ] milk: 4 lbs.—nonfat dry and evaporated (or this can be liquid soy or rice milk

- [ ] sugars: 15 lbs.—Granulated, brown, molasses, honey, jams and preserves, fruit drink, flavored gelatin

- [ ] dry yeast: $1/4$ lb.; baking soda: $1/4$ lb.; baking powder: $1/2$ lb.; vinegar: $1/2$ gal.; iodized salt: 4 lbs.

Additional food items:

- [ ] canned foods (two-to-three-year shelf life)
- [ ] dehydrated foods (three-to-four year shelf life)
- [ ] freeze-dried foods in pouches (two-to-four-year shelf life)
- [ ] freeze-dried food rations in cans (ten to fifteen-year shelf life)
- [ ] beef and turkey jerky
- [ ] bouillon cubes
- [ ] cheese, canned or in powder form
- [ ] coffee
- [ ] condiments—ketchup, mustard, soy sauce, mayonnaise, BBQ sauce in individual packets, if possible
- [ ] powdered eggs
- [ ] powdered-drink mixes such as Kool-Aid
- [ ] seasonings
- [ ] tea
- [ ] textured vegetable protein (TVP)

Don't forget that some food supply houses offer package deals for one-month, six-month, and one-year supplies of food, balanced nutritionally. This takes the guesswork out of planning.

3

Cooking Equipment

In an emergency if you have to set up housekeeping somewhere other than in your own kitchen, you'll find what you need in most camping stores. If you're preparing for a longer-term arrangement, in which you will be preparing food rather than just eating it out of MRE containers or camping pouches, you will need to select essential items for your style of cooking. Don't forget baby bottles and whatever special supplies you will need to care for an infant or pets.

- ☐ airtight food-storage containers to keep perishable items dry and pest-free

- ☐ aluminum foil—heavy-duty for cooking, regular strength for storage

- ☐ baggies

- ☐ baking tins or glass—cake pans, pie plates, bread pans, cookie sheets

- ☐ bowls, several sizes

- ☐ butter churn, molds

- [ ] can openers, manual types
- [ ] canning supplies
  - [ ] funnel with wide bottom
  - [ ] jars
  - [ ] lids and rings
  - [ ] lifter for jars
  - [ ] pressure cooker
  - [ ] racks
  - [ ] tongs
  - [ ] wrenches for jars
- [ ] cheesecloth
- [ ] coffee filters
- [ ] coffee percolator
- [ ] cooler, ice chest
- [ ] corks
- [ ] dehydrators, electric and hanging
- [ ] dipper
- [ ] dishpan, dishwashing soap
- [ ] dutch oven
- [ ] egg beater, hand-crank type
- [ ] fireplace tools
- [ ] flour sifter
- [ ] frying pans, assorted sizes, with lids

- ☐ funnel

- ☐ gloves (rubber, plastic)

- ☐ grater/slicers for vegetables and cheeses

- ☐ grinders for grain, meat (hand and electric)

- ☐ hot pads

- ☐ juice extractor

- ☐ kettle

- ☐ knives

  - ☐ butcher
  - ☐ meat cleaver
  - ☐ paring knives
  - ☐ skinning knives with curved blades
  - ☐ utility knives, smooth and serrated

- ☐ ladles

- ☐ lids, gamma type for plastic buckets

- ☐ liquid measuring cups

- ☐ measuring cups and spoons

- ☐ napkins, paper

- ☐ newspapers (for temporary table covers)

- ☐ noodle maker, hand-cranked

- ☐ nutcracker

- ☐ paper towels

☐ paper plates and plastic utensils

☐ peelers

☐ potato masher

☐ pots and pans

  ☐ casserole dishes
  ☐ casserole pan, covered
  ☐ drain bowl (colander)
  ☐ griddle, flat cast-iron type
  ☐ grill for cooking over open fire
  ☐ kettles
  ☐ pitchers
  ☐ roaster
  ☐ saucepans, two-quart, three-quart, with lids

☐ rolling pin

☐ scouring pads

☐ sieve

☐ spatulas, metal and plastic

☐ spoons, assorted, wooden and plastic

☐ stockpots, with lids

☐ thermoses

☐ timer

☐ tongs

☐ towels

- [ ] trivets—especially round ones that can be used on a wood stove to allow for Dutch-oven cooking

- [ ] utensils/plates/glasses/place settings

- [ ] wax paper

- [ ] whisks

- [ ] wide-mouth funnel

Note: cast-iron cookware is preferable for wood-stove cooking.

4

Water Management

Experts generally agree that emergency provisions should include a minimum of one gallon of water per person per day (half a gallon for drinking, half for cleaning up).

Containers:

☐ barrels, 55-gallon size—clean, preferably new and unused

☐ pails, jugs for carrying and storing water—clean, preferably unused

☐ hard plastic soda bottles (two-liter size) for storing water. These should be thoroughly washed and rinsed. Don't recycle plastic milk bottles or cartons, since these have been designed to be biodegradable.

☐ hoses

☐ pots in which to boil water

☐ hand pump

☐ purifying chemicals (iodine crystals, unscented chlorine bleach—we use a product called Aerobic 7)

☐ medicine dropper for dispensing purifying
     chemicals

☐ purifying filters—There are many. We use Katadyn filters in
     several sizes

☐ siphon tube

☐ funnel

Save rainwater if you have the place for a barrel. Rainwater
may come in handy for bathing. Also, if you use it to take a bath,
some can be salvaged to flush the toilet. Another possible source
of water in an emergency might be a water bed—not for drinking, but for bathing, flushing toilets, and so forth.

Fill up bathtubs and other containers with water before New
Year's Eve.

Sanitary Supplies

As a nation, we are great buyers of cleansers for ourselves and our homes. In emergency conditions, it may be hard to maintain cleanliness in your food preparation and waste disposal. But keeping clean helps you and your family to stay healthy, so it's worth whatever work it takes.

Key cleaning and sanitary items:

☐ ammonia

☐ bags, plastic trash in various sizes, especially large black garbage bags

☐ borax for waste treatment

☐ broom and dustpan

☐ buckets (metal and plastic)

☐ chlorine bleach (unscented) or other disinfectant

☐ cleansers (Comet, Bon Ami)

☐ clothesline rope (those who routinely line-dry their clothing may be interested to know there are now solar-powered clothesline poles; see the Real Goods entry in the products and services section, page 157.

- ☐ deodorizer

- ☐ detergents and soaps—for dishwashing, laundry, and cleaning counters and tables

- ☐ dish cloths

- ☐ drain cleaner

- ☐ flea collars, soap and powder

- ☐ fly swatter

- ☐ insect repellent

- ☐ lime (large bags) for waste treatment

- ☐ Lysol or similar disinfectant

- ☐ mops and plastic sponges

- ☐ paper towels

- ☐ plunger

- ☐ rodent poisons and traps

- ☐ sanitary napkins, diapers, adult incontinence pads

- ☐ toilet paper—as much as you have room to store

- ☐ trash cans (plastic with lids for waste, and separate ones for storage of supplies and equipment; the tighter the lids, the better)

☐ tubs for washing and rinsing clothing

☐ tubs for dishes

☐ washboard

☐ wringer, manual

6

Medicines

These lists may seem intimidating because they are so long, but no one is going to need everything here. This is intended as a checklist—a list to be *checked*, not followed slavishly.

Medical equipment. Note: Instead of assembling your own supplies, you might consider buying a prestocked first-aid kit. This item is available in pharmacies, camping stores, survival-supply houses, catalogues of safety gear, and so on. Further, add your personal items to this prepared list, to have at the ready for any emergency. If you are going to be in an area where snake bite is a possibility, it would be wise to get a snake-bite kit.

☐ bedpan

☐ blood pressure cuff

☐ instant cold packs and hot packs

☐ enema bag (reusable equipment)

☐ hand mirror

☐ magnifying glass

- ☐ medicine droppers
- ☐ surgical masks
- ☐ disposable rubber or latex gloves
- ☐ cotton swabs
- ☐ oral thermometer
- ☐ penlight
- ☐ safety pins
- ☐ scissors
- ☐ tweezers
- ☐ forceps for removing small objects
- ☐ irrigation syringe with plastic tip
- ☐ thermometer and case
- ☐ bandages (assorted sizes and shapes; these items are frequently on sale, so consider laying in a supply when you have a chance)
  - ☐ ace bandages
  - ☐ butterfly closures
  - ☐ triangular bandages
  - ☐ pressure bandages
  - ☐ gauze bandages
  - ☐ sterile dressings, 4" × 4"
  - ☐ adhesive tape
  - ☐ nonadherent dressings
  - ☐ absorbent cotton

☐ moleskin for blistered feet
☐ sanitary napkins are excellent compresses for serious injuries
☐ clear plastic food wrap (it makes an excellent nonstick bandage; it can be boiled until sterile, cooled, and then put on a burn)

Obviously, if you have a medical condition that requires injections, ask your doctor for a prescription for a sufficient quantity of syringes. You can't buy these over the counter in most places.

Oral medicines, prescriptions, and over-the-counter medications. Pay attention to expiration dates, and replace medications that have lost their potency.

Note: Ask your pharmacist for advice on brands. The ones named here are only suggestions, based on my wife's and my own experiences.

☐ allergy pills

☐ antacids (such as Pepto-Bismol, Pepcid AC, Zantac 45)

☐ antibiotics

☐ antidiarrheal tablets and liquids (Kaopectate, Immodium AD)

☐ antihistamines

☐ aspirin

☐ charcoal/carbon dust for use as antidotes

- [ ] cough suppressants

- [ ] decongestant pills and sprays, such as Sudafed

- [ ] earaches (Mullein drops)

- [ ] iodine pills for purifying water

- [ ] Ipecac syrup

- [ ] laxatives

- [ ] lozenges

- [ ] mineral oil

- [ ] motion-sickness pills (ginger pills also work well)

- [ ] mouthwash

- [ ] No-Doz (there may be occasions when it's particularly important to stay awake and alert)

- [ ] oil of cloves for a toothache

- [ ] pain relievers (such as Tylenol, Advil, Ibuprofen, Aleve, Motrin)

- [ ] piperazine, a dewormer

- [ ] potassium iodide (anti-radiation exposure)

- [ ] predisone, if prescribed by your physician

- [ ] prescription drugs (ones your physician has already prescribed; ask him or her for a prescription for Isuprel, an antishock medication)

- [ ] Children's Tylenol

☐ rehydration items (Epsom salts, Pediolyte powder to restore electrolytes lost through perspiration; Gatorade is good for this, and oral rehydration packets are available as well)

☐ Sleeping pills

Topical medicines. Fluids, salves, and creams kept in medicine cabinets or first-aid kits should be checked at regular intervals—every couple of months—to be sure none has expired.

☐ ammonia

☐ antifungal cream

☐ antibiotic ointment

☐ antiseptic solution, such as Betadine

☐ baking soda

☐ calamine lotion

☐ cortisone itch cream

☐ eyewash

☐ first aid creams (such as Betadine, Neosporin, Mycetracin, Johnson & Johnson)

☐ hydrogen peroxide

☐ insect bites remedies (calamine lotion or cream, Camphophenique)

☐ isopropyl alcohol

☐ mercurochrome

☐ ophthalmic ointment (such as Neosporin)

☐ sunblock (choose the highest SPF possible)

☐ sunburn lotion

☐ petroleum jelly

☐ tincture of benzoin

Baby care. Parents are usually well aware of the supplies they need, such as disposable diapers, baby oil, disinfectant, lotion, shampoo, diaper rash ointment, cornstarch, and so on. Ask your pediatrician for information on emergency preparedness for infants and children.

7

Light and Heat

The following supplies are of very great importance to the safety and comfort of your family. If you find you have overstocked on any item, bear in mind that almost everything on this list is useful for barter.

Note: There should be no open flames in a house without someone watching—even candles. In an emergency, when it's dark, go to bed—extinguish lights unless there is an injured person.

The cheapest, oldest lighting:

- [ ] candles (buy in quantity, especially long-burning votive candles available in grocery stores)

- [ ] waterproof matches, wooden matches

- [ ] magnifying glass for use in making fire (concentrating the sun's rays on a flammable object will give a fire a start)

- [ ] candle molds and wicks (candle drippings and stubs of candles can be recycled—this would be an excellent do-it-yourself project activity to do) with children, putting them in touch with frontier times)

The lighting basics:

☐ flashlights (every member of the family should have one beside the bed, with extras in such places as the kitchen, garage, basement, and near stairs)

☐ extra flashlight bulbs

☐ coleman lanterns, battery, oil, kerosene

☐ solar rechargeable lanterns

☐ batteries (AAA, AA, C, D, 9V, lantern, and so on; consider buying the more expensive but more durable NiCad-type battery; unlike alkaline batteries that can only be recharged if you catch them before they are 50 percent depleted; NiCads can be recharged even if they are dead)

☐ solar-powered battery recharger

☐ light bulbs

☐ light sticks

Heating basics:

☐ generators
    ☐ gasoline, diesel, or propane
    ☐ stoves
    ☐ propane stove
    ☐ multifuel stove with box oven
    ☐ solar stove/oven
    ☐ wood stove
    ☐ AA-battery powered Zip stove

- ☐ sterno (recommend at least twelve two-hour cans)
- ☐ disposable lighters
- ☐ lighters and lighter fluid
- ☐ magnesium fire-starter
- ☐ fire extinguisher, ABC type

8

Clothing and Bedding

Layered clothing is the key to keeping warm, and the same applies to bedding—wearing socks and sweaters to bed can trap body heat and keep you warm through the night.

Clothing you will need. Get extra sets of warm clothing, particularly underwear and socks; you won't have to do laundry so often, thereby saving water. Here's a list of the essentials:

- ☐ sweaters in various weights, long- and short-sleeved, so you will be able to adjust your temperature, putting on more or taking them off

- ☐ cotton shirts, long- and short-sleeved

- ☐ extra sets of underwear, regular and thermal

- ☐ coats in various weights—light, medium, heavy

- ☐ parkas and anoraks

- ☐ sweatshirts and sweatpants

- ☐ slacks, particularly corduroy (jeans are good to work in but won't keep you warm)

- [ ] socks (a variety of weights in cotton and wool; wearing two pairs to bed is a surefire route to warm feet)

- [ ] overalls (farm type and mechanic type)

- [ ] headgear for winter (woolen caps, headache bands, ear muffs, and so on; summer hats with wide brims, caps with visors)

- [ ] gloves (various weights, work gloves, woolen winter gloves, mittens)

- [ ] footwear
  - [ ] heavy work shoes, boots
  - [ ] rubber boots or galoshes
  - [ ] running shoes, tennis shoes, hightops, and so on

Clothing care and repair. To keep your possessions in good condition, check these items:

- [ ] adhesive (builder's glue) to patch shoes

- [ ] clothes basket or hamper

- [ ] irons (the antique, nonelectric kind can be heated on the stove; also electric irons, if power is available; however, in times of emergency, the "pressed look" is probably the first thing to go; it's not essential)

- [ ] laces for boots and shoes

- [ ] leather conditioning—polish, saddle soap

- ☐ extra heels and soles

- ☐ sewing kit
  - ☐ awl, rug hook
  - ☐ bobbins
  - ☐ buttons
  - ☐ iron-on patches
  - ☐ knitting needles, crochet hook
  - ☐ needles, sewing machine (in various sizes), and upholstery
  - ☐ pins
  - ☐ tape measure
  - ☐ thread (large spools of cotton, nylon, and polyester threads in a variety of colors)
  - ☐ velcro
  - ☐ waterproofing spray for clothing

- ☐ sewing machine (the nonelectric, treadle type)

- ☐ soaps and laundry detergents

Bedding, linen, and towels:

- ☐ Arctic sleeping bags for the whole family (get advice from an experienced camper, at a camping goods store, or check catalogs; sleeping bags are rated for different temperatures; be sure to get ones suitable for your region)

- ☐ blankets (all types, including wool, cotton, quilted; also thermal blankets and reflective blankets)

☐ pillows

☐ sheets, pillowcases

☐ towels (all sizes), washcloths, and bathmats

9

Automotive Supplies

Most of us simply jump into our cars without a second thought about emergency preparedness. A spare tire and jack usually come with the vehicle. AAA may not be an option, so learn to change a tire, if you don't already know how. The following list may seem like a lot of "stuff," but there are times when we need to give assistance as well as handling our own situations.

Automotive emergency supplies:

- ☐ flashlight with extra batteries

- ☐ jumper cables

- ☐ fire extinguisher (5 lb., ABC type)

- ☐ locking gas-cap

- ☐ spare tire (checked for readiness)

- ☐ portable jack

- ☐ tire repair kit and pump/emergency tire inflator

- ☐ flares

☐ folding shovel

☐ first-aid kit and manual (including sunscreen—you might have to walk for help)

☐ bottled water and nonperishable, high-energy snack foods

☐ thermal blanket

☐ maps

Garage supplies. Keep the following items on hand for seasonal changes, or take them along if any trip you plan is likely to run into rough conditions or be far from service stations.

☐ utility light

☐ batteries (store dry batteries and acid batteries separately)

☐ antifreeze

☐ brake fluid

☐ brake parts

☐ extra headlamps

☐ transmission fluid

☐ jumper cables

☐ sparkplugs

☐ fuses

☐ drive belt

- [ ] windshield-washer fluid

- [ ] wiper blades

- [ ] filters (air, gas, oil)

- [ ] fuels
  - [ ] starter fluid
  - [ ] case of oil (10W40)
  - [ ] gasoline (two or more chemically stabilized five-gallon cans; will retain full potency about thirty days without additives)

- [ ] all-season tires

- [ ] manual air pump

- [ ] chains

- [ ] log/tow chain

- [ ] floor jack

- [ ] grease gun

1 0

Building Repair

Many homeowners are accustomed to doing their own repairs and so will probably already have most of the items on this list that they are likely to need. However, in times of emergency stores often run short of supplies, so stock up now on anything you have been meaning to get.

- ☐ block and tackle
- ☐ caulk (siliconized)
- ☐ cord (para 550# test, 200 yards)
- ☐ cord (twine 600 yards)
- ☐ electronics
    - ☐ adapters
    - ☐ copper-to-aluminum splice kits
    - ☐ extension cords (three-prong)
    - ☐ fuses for home, auto, and other
    - ☐ soldering kit
    - ☐ splices (wire nut)
    - ☐ wire gauge/cutter/stripper

- ☐ wire (household current)
    - ☐ fasteners
    - ☐ anchors for masonry and wallboard
    - ☐ nails, general purpose
    - ☐ rivets
    - ☐ screws for wood and metal
    - ☐ tacks (carpet)

- ☐ work gloves

- ☐ glue (epoxy, wood glue, super glue)

- ☐ hand truck

- ☐ hose

- ☐ knife sharpener

- ☐ ladders

- ☐ level

- ☐ oil can

- ☐ plastic, rolls of clear plastic for emergency window repair

- ☐ rope (2000# test)

- ☐ ruler (straight-edge)

- ☐ sandpaper (various grades from coarse to fine)

- ☐ saws (bow, chain, coping, cross-cut, hacksaw, keyhole, jig)

- ☐ scraper

- ☐ screwdrivers (flexible, offset, straight slot, Phillips head)

- ☐ snake for drain
- ☐ steel wool
- ☐ tape (duct, electrical)
- ☐ tape measure
- ☐ tar for sealing roof
- ☐ tin snips
- ☐ tools (hand, not electrically powered)
  - ☐ axes, wedges to use with the ax, replacement heads
  - ☐ chisels for wood and metal
  - ☐ drill (hand-driven, geared, with drill bits for wood, masonry, and metal)
  - ☐ eye and ear protectors
  - ☐ flashlight
  - ☐ hammers (ball peen, construction, mallet, tack)
  - ☐ pipe cutter, threader, bender
  - ☐ pliers (bolt cutters, electrical, locking, regular, needle nose)

Gardening Tools and Supplies

You don't have to have acres of land to garden. You can grow any number of foods right on a ledge in an apartment. You do need adequate sunlight and water. But you can catch rainwater rather than using your stored water. For those who want to get serious about growing food, try to buy only nonhybrid seed. You can save the seeds from these plants and grow them year after year. A 50-foot-by-100-foot plot will grow the vegetables for a small family. Unless you are going into full-scale food production, you really don't need a lot of paraphernalia.

You will need weeding tools, of which there are a great variety. Check out your local nursery or call for one of the gardening catalogues listed in the Products and Sources section of this book.

☐ chainsaw

☐ compost fork

☐ digging forks

☐ digging spades

- ☐ fencing
  - ☐ barbed
  - ☐ chickenwire
  - ☐ electric fence (battery-powered and solar-powered)
  - ☐ square wire
- ☐ hoes
- ☐ lawnmower (push-type)
- ☐ pick
- ☐ posthole diggers (rotating and pincher)
- ☐ pruning shears
- ☐ rakes, leaf, and rocks
- ☐ rototiller
- ☐ scythe
- ☐ shovels (large and small spades, round-nosed snow shovels)
- ☐ sickel
- ☐ sledgehammer
- ☐ trimming shears
- ☐ trowels
- ☐ wagon (four-wheel)
- ☐ weed eater
- ☐ wheelbarrows (two)
- ☐ wire (binding)

1 2

Hunting Equipment

Whether or not you own or decide to acquire a firearm for hunting or self-defense has everything to do with your values, vision, and location. Hunting game is widely practiced by people who live in the country and small towns. One is not going to find deer or game birds in the cities. A shotgun to protect your home is one thing, a deer-hunting rifle is another. Handguns (which require permits to buy and to carry) raise their own set of questions.

The following are some considerations for those thinking of getting trained in firearm use and safety and who plan to hunt wild game in the locality in which they live. (And bear in mind that experienced hunters are successful less than 25 percent of the time.)

Firearms for the type of game you are hunting. There is a wide array of choices available for any hunting firearm. A first visit to a gun shop can be daunting. You should ask to see the following and compare their features with comparable guns by other manufacturers before making a final selection:

- [ ] .22 rifle—Ruger 10/22

- [ ] pump shotgun (12 or 20 gauge)
  - [ ] Remington 870 Wing Master
  - [ ] Remington 1100 Youth
  - [ ] Mossberg M500/590

- [ ] hunting rifle
  - [ ] Remington Seven Ultra Lite .308
  - [ ] Ruger 77/44

- [ ] hunting rifle (semiautomatic)
  - [ ] Ruger Mini–14
  - [ ] Colt AR15

- [ ] M1A Springfield Armory

Scopes, spare parts, amounts of ammunition, and accessories are also your personal decision.

Any decision on owning a weapon, and which one, should be based on your own research and philosophy.

Bibliography

Overviews for the Average Reader

YOURDON, EDWARD AND YOURDON, JENNIFER, *Time Bomb 2000: What the Year 2000 Computer Crisis Means to You*, Prentice-Hall, Upper Saddle River, New Jersey, 1998. ISBN 0–13–095284–2.

The best single volume overview of the problem and its possible impacts during different time periods by one of the world's leading software authorities and his daughter. Ed Yourdon is the author of twenty-five computer books and texts. If you are only going to read one book, this is the one.

HYATT, MICHAEL S., *The Millennium Bug: How to Survive the Coming Chaos*, Regnery Publishing, Washington, D.C., 1998. ISBN 0–89526–373–4.

This engaging work is an insightful reinforcement to the Yourdon book from another perspective, reaching parallel conclusions.

REEVE, SIMON, AND COLIN McGHEE, *The Millennium Bomb: Countdown to a £400 Billion Catastrophe*, Satin Publications,

London, UK, 1996. ISBN 1–901250–00–8.

Written in 1996, this book provides vivid coverage of the problem by two British journalists. Their book is valuable for its breadth, historical coverage, and readability.

Your Finances

KEYES, TONY, *The Year 2000 Computer Crisis: An Investor's Survival Guide*, 1997, Brookdale, Maryland ISBN 1–9658939–0–1.

The first and only book to date to provide thoughtful analysis of the issue, its financial implications, and suggest personal strategies.

Personal Concerns

LORD, JIM, *A Survival Guide for the Year 2000 Problem: How to Save Yourself from the Most Deadly Screw-Up in History*, J. Marion Publishing, Bowie, Maryland, 1997. ISBN 0–9660200–0–6.

A pioneer in Y2K awareness, Lord was out in front with this book (and his newsletter), describing the problem in a down-to-earth fashion and recommending practical responses.

MORRIS, J. R., *Year 2000 Personal Protection Guide: How to Protect Your Assets, Identity, and Credit from the Upcoming Millennium Bug Computer Crisis*, Sterlingmore Publications, Abilene, Texas, 1998. ISBN 0–9663988–3–1.

A small-business owner and CPA, Morris provides the most

extensive list of essential documents and action steps for getting your financial and other legal records in shape for the year 2000.

SUNSET RESEARCH GROUP, *How to Survive and Prosper After the Year 2000 Computer Crash*, Sunset Research Group, 8918 W. 21st St. N., # 200–224, Wichita, Kansas 67205. No ISBN.

A concise, fifty-two-page analysis with specific recommendations for surviving a projected major and long-term societal disaster as a result of Y2K. No ISBN.

KELLY, JASON, *Y2K: It's Already Too Late*, Jason Kelly Press, Los Angeles, California, 1998. ISBN 0–9664387–0–1.

A military technothriller with a pronounced Y2K overlay. Although this is a novel, the scenarios described are far too possible to be dismissed.

TIGGRE, DON, L., *Y2K: The Millenium Bug*, Xlibras, Princeton, NJ, 1998. Phone: 1–888–7XLIBRAS.

A multilevel novel that plays out the aftermath of Y2K in the lives of several characters.

Your PC or Small Business

FLETCHER, MICHAEL, *Computer Crisis 2000*, Self-Counsel Press, North Vancouver, BC, 1998. ISBN 1–55180–138–8

A brief but thorough action plan for getting a Y2K project off the ground quickly, of particular value to smaller businesses and governmental entitites.

BOURNE, K. C., *Year 2000 Solutions for Dummies*, IDG Books Worldwide, Foster City, California, 1997. ISBN 0–7645–0241–7.

Despite its off-putting title, this is a very accessible introduction and action plan outline for small to medium businesses.

FULLER, JESSE AND BUTLER, BARBARA, *Finding and Fixing Your Year 2000 Problem: A Guide for Small Businesses and Organizations*, Academic Press, San Diego, California, 1998. ISBN 0–12–251335–5.

An extensively detailed and comprehensive project design and management for smaller organizations.

Legal Considerations

SCOTT, MICHAEL AND WARDEN, REID, *The Year 2000 Computer Crisis: Law, Business, and Technology*, Little Falls, NJ, Glasser Legal Works, 1998. ISBN 1–888075–82–1.

Contracts, litigation, and liability. It's all here.

The Big Picture for the Technically Oriented

COWLES, RICK, *Electric Utilities and Y2K*, *EUY2K*, Penns Grove, New Jersey, 1998. ISBN 0–966–3402–13.

The core infrastructure upon which modern society depends is electricity. This is the book to read to understand its vulnerability to Y2K and problems associated with its generation and distribution.

JONES, CAPERS, *The Year 2000 Software Problem: Quantifying the Costs and Assessing the Consequences*, ACM Press, New York, New York, 1998. ISBN 0–201–30964–5.

A renowned expert on software productivity and measurement spells out his chilling worldwide assessment of the problem and probable failure rates.

DE JAGER, PETER & BERGEON, RICHARD, *Managing 00: Surviving the Year 2000 Computing Crisis*, Wiley Publishing, New York, 1997. ISBN 0–471–17937–X.

The Paul Reveres of the Y2K-awareness movement, they have created an important and valuable resource for any manager seeking to get a better understanding of the problem and the actions needed to address it.

KAPPELMAN, LEON, ED., *Year 2000 Problem: Strategies and Solutions from the Fortune 1,000*, International Thomson Computer Press, Boston, Massachusetts, 1997. ISBN 1–85302–913–3.

This valuable 450-page anthology brings together some of the best writers on the subject available up to 1997.

ULRICH, WILLIAM, AND HAYES, IAN, *The Year 2000 Software Crisis: Challenge of the Century*, Yourdon Press/Prentice Hall, Upper Saddle River, New Jersey, 1997. ISBN 0–13–655664–7.

ULRICH, WILLIAM, & HAYES, IAN, *The Year 2000 Software Crisis: The Continuing Challenge*, Yourdon Press/Prentice Hall, Upper Saddle River, New Jersey, 1998. ISBN 0–13–960154–6.

Any member of a top management team concerned with Y2K issues and projects should have these books. They provide risk-management and legal strategies; supply chain and embedded-systems solutions; contingency planning, triage, and crisis management; and testing and project-planning resources.

PUTTING Y2K IN CONTEXT

I have found the books in this section to be a great value for putting Y2K into broader context. They are more scholarly than popular in their approach.

Technology

GILDER, GEORGE, *Microcosm: The Quantum Revolution in Economics and Technology*, Simon and Shuster, New York, 1989. ISBN 0–671–540969–1.

ELLUL, JACQUES, *The Technological Bluff*, Eerdmans, Grand Rapids, Michigan, 1990. ISBN 0-8028–3678–X.

TENNER, EDWARD, *Why Things Bite Back: Technology and the Revenge of Unintended Consequences*, Alfred A. Knopf, New York, 1996. ISBN 0–679–42563–2.

PETERSON, IVARS, *Fatal Defect: Chasing Killer Computer Bugs*, Vintage Books, New York 1996. ISBN 0–8129–2023–6.

Economics

DAVIDSON, JAMES DALE AND REES-MOGG, WILLIAM, *The Great Reckoning: How the World Will Change in the Depression of the 1990s*, Simon & Shuster, New York, 1991. ISBN 0–671–66980–X.

FISHER, DAVID, *The Great Wave: Price Revolitions and the Rhythm of History,* Oxford University Press, New York, 1996. ISBN 0–19–505377–X.

GALBRAITH, JOHN KENNETH, *The Great Crash 1929,* Houghton Mifflin, New York, 1997. ISBN 0–395–85999–9.

KINDLEBERGER, CHARLES P., *Manias, Panics, and Crashes: A History of Financial Crises,* Basic Books, New York, 1978. ISBN 0–465–04402–6.

KOSARES, MICHAEL J., *The ABCs of Gold Investing,* Addicus Books, Omaha, Nebraska, 1997. ISBN 1–886039–29–1.

PRECHTER, ROBERT, *At the Crest of the Tidal Wave: A Forecast for the Great Bear Market,* New Classics Library, 1996. ISBN 093275097.

ROTHBARD, MURRAY, *The Mystery of Banking,* Richardson & Snyder, New York, 1983. ISBN 0–943940–04–4.

ROTHBARD, MURRAY, *America's Great Depression,* Sheed and Ward, Kansas City, 1975. ISBN 0–8362–0647–9.

ROTHSCHILD, JOHN, *The Bear Book: Survive and Profit in Ferocious Markets,* Wiley, New York, 1998. ISBN 0–471–19718–1.

SARLOS, ANDREW, *Fear, Greed, and the End of the Rainbow: Guarding Your Assets in the Coming Bear Market,* Key Porter Books, Toronto, Canada. ISBN 1–55013–896–0.

Socio-Cultural Studies

MCNEILL, WILLIAM H., *The Global Condition: Conquerors, Catastrophes, and Community,* Princeton University Press, New Jersey, 1993. ISBN 0691025592.

SOROKIN, PITIRIM, *The Crisis of Our Age, One World,* Oxford, UK, 1941. ISBN 1–85168–028–4.

SOROKIN, PITIRIM, *Man and Society in Calamity,* E. F. Dulton, New York, 1942. No ISBN.

STRAUSS, WILLIAM AND HOWE, NEIL, *The Fourth Turning: An American Prophecy*, Broadway Books, New York, New York, 1997. ISBN 0–553–06682–X.

TAINTER, JOSEPH, *The Collapse of Complex Societies*, Cambridge University Press, Cambridge, UK, 1988. ISBN 0–321–38673–X.

Disaster Recovery

DRABEK, THOMAS & HOELMA, *Gerard, Emergency Management: Principles and Practice for Local Government*, International City Management Association, Washington, DC, 1991. ISBN 0–87326–082–1.

DYNES, RUSSELL AND TIERNEY, KATHLEEN, EDS., *Disasters, Collective Behavior, and Social Organization*, Associated University Presses, Canbury, New Jersey, 1994. ISBN 0–87413–498–6.

TOIGO, JON, *Disaster Recovery Planning: For Computers and Communications Resources*, Wiley & Sons, New York, 1996. ISBN 0–471–12175–4.

Community

ANDREWS, DAVE, *Building a Better World: Developing Communities of Hope in Troubled Times*, Abington Press, 1998. ISBN 0824517261.

EHRENHALT, ALAN, *The Lost City: The Forgotten Virtues of Community in America*, Basic Books, New York, 1996. ISBN 0465041930.

HESS, KARL, *Community Technology*, Loompanics Unlimited, Port Townsend, Washington, 1979. ISBN 1–55950–131–6.

HESSELBEIN, FRANCES, ED., *The Community of the Future* (Drucker

Foundation Future Series), Simon & Shuster, New York, 1998. ISBN 0787910066.

HENTON, DOUGLAS, ED., *Grassroots Leaders for a New Economy: How Civic Entrepreneurs are Building Prosperous Communities*, Jossey Bass, 1997. ISBN 0787908274.

HYNES, H. PATRICIA, *A Patch of Eden: America's Inner City Gardeners*, Chelsea Green Publishing, 1996. ISBN 0930031806.

KREITZMAN, JOHN & MCKNIGHT, JOHN, *Building Communities from the Inside Out: A Path Toward Finding and Mobilizing a Community's Assets*, Acta Publications, 1997. ISBN 87946108X.

MCKNIGHT, JOHN, *The Careless Society: Community and its Counterfeits*, Basic Books, New York, 1996. ISBN 0465091261.

NISBET, ROBERT, A., *The Question for Community*, Oxford Unversity Press, NY, 1953. ISBN 0–19500703–4.

SHUMAN, MICHAEL H., *Going Local: Creating Self-Reliant Communities in a Global Age*, The Free Press, New York, New York, 1998. ISBN 0–684–83012–4.

THEOBALD, ROBERT, *Reworking Success: New Communities at the Millennium*, New Society Publishers, Stoney Creek, Connecticut, 1997. ISBN 0–86571–367–7.

Self-Reliant Living

ASHWORTH, SUZANNE, *Seed to Seed: Seed Saving Techniques for the Vegetable Gardener*, Seed Saver Publications, Decorah, Iowa, 1991. ISBN 0–9613977–7–2.

Basic Self-Reliance, The Church of Jesus Christ of Latter Day Saints, Salt Lake City, Utah, 1989. No ISBN.

BROWN, TOM, *Field Guide to Suburban Survival,* Berkeley Books, New York, 1984. ISBN 0–425–10572–4.

BROWN, TOM, *Field Guide to Wilderness Survival,* Berkeley Books, New York, 1983. ISBN 0–425–10572–5.

ELLIS, BARBARA W. AND BRADLEY, FERN MARSHALL, *The Organic Gardener's Handbook of Natural Insect and Disease Control,* Rodale Press, Emmaus, Pennsylvania, 1996. ISBN 0–87596–753–1.

EMERY, CARLA, *The Encyclopedia of Country Living: An Old-Fashioned Recipe Book,* Sasquatch Books, Seattle, Washington, 1994. ISBN 0–912365–95–1.

EVANGELISTA, ANITA, *How to Develop a Low-Cost Family Food Storage System,* Loompanics Unlimited, Port Townsend, Washington, 1995. ISBN 1–55950–130–8.

EVANGELISTA, ANITA, *Backyard Meat Production: How to Grow All the Meat You Need in Your Own Backyard,* Loompanics Unlimited, Port Townsend, Washington, 1997. ISBN 1–55950–168–5.

GUIDETTI, GERI WELZEL, *Build Your Ark: How to Prepare for Self-Reliance in Uncertain Times,* The Ark Institute, Monkton, Maryland, 1996. ISBN 0–938928–01–5.

INGRAM, DAVE, *Guide to Emergency Survival Communications,* Universal Electronics, Columbus, Ohio, 1997. ISBN 0–916661–05–9.

JACOB, JEFFREY, *New Pioneers: The Back to the Land Movement and the Search for a Sustainable Future,* Penn State University Press, University Park, Pennsylvania, 1997. ISBN 0–271–01621–3.

KAINS, M. G., *Five Acres and Independence,* Dover, New York, New York, 1973. ISBN 0–486–20974.

KOURIK, ROBERT, *Designing and Maintaining Your Edible Landscape Naturally*, Metamorphic Press, Santa Rosa, California, 1986. ISBN 0–9615848–0–7.

LARSON, KEN, *Becoming Self-Reliant: How to Become Less Dependent on Society and Government*, Rhema Publishing, Suwanee, Georgia, 1997. ISBN 0–9642497–1–5.

MOLLISON, BILL, *Introduction to Permaculture*, Tagan Publications, Tyalguam, Australia, 1991. ISBN 0–908228– 08–2.

POISSON, LEANDRE AND POISSON, GRETCHEN VOGEL, *Solar Gardening: Growing Vegetables Year-Round the American Intensive Way*, Chelsea Green Publishing Company, White River Junction, Vermont, 1994. ISBN 0–930031–69–5.

ROBINSON, ED AND CAROLYN, *The Have More Plan*, Storey Communications, Pownal, Vermont, 1973. ISBN 0–88266–024–1.

SOUTH, J. ALLAN, *The Sense of Survival*, Timpanogos Publishers, Orem, Utah, 1990. ISBN 0-935329–00–0.

STEVENS, JAMES TALMAGE, *Making the Best of Basics: Family-Preparedness Handbook*, Gold Leaf Press, Seattle, Washington, 1997. ISBN 1–882723–25–2.

SCHWENKE, KARL, *Successful Small-Scale Farming: An Organic Approach*, Storey Communications, Pownal, Vermont, 1979. ISBN 0–88266–642–8.

THOMSEN, SKIP AND FRESHWATER, CAT, *The Modern Homestead Manual*, Pandanus Publishing, Pahoa, Hawaii, 1994. ISBN 0–9625960–4–3.

U.S. Department of the Army, *U.S. Army Survival Manual*, FM 21–76, Dorset Press, New York, 1998. ISBN 1–56619–022–3.

Annotated Websites
My Top Sites

There are hundreds of Websites focused on Y2K. Here is a list of the ones I have found myself visiting daily and weekly. There are many other excellent sites.

Westergaard Year 2000 (www.y2ktimebomb.com)

A webzine with a stable of columnists posting new information and commentary every weekday on a wide array of Y2K topics.

The year 2000 Information Center (www.year2000.com)

Peter deJager's site. Very comprehensive. Check their daily press-clippings section for Y2K articles appearing around the world in the English-language.

Gary North's Y2K Links & Forums (www.garynorth.com)

Both the most extensive set of Y2K documents collected and commented on by category and among the most dire of forecasts. Dr. North is an economic historian and theologian.

Alan Simpson's Comlinks.com (www.comlinks.com)

Alan Simpson has been at the forefront of raising Y2K issues. His site has valuable information and frequent updates.

Infrastructure Defense (www.y2ktoday.com)

James Adams, author of The Next World War: Computers Are the Weapons, *resigned as CEO of UPI to create this organization and run this Website of current news on Y2K and America's infrastructure.*

Y2K News Magazine (www.y2knews.com)

A biweekly posting of both reprints and original articles on Y2K.

Ed Yourdon's Home Page (wwwyourdon.com)

Excellent resource. His latest thinking, articles, book revisions, and an on-line discussion group.

Dr. Ed Yardeni's Economic Network (www.yardeni.com)

The chief economist of Deutsche Bank Securities in New York is one of the leading authorities on the probable impact of Y2K on the global economy. Essential.

The Cassandra Project (http://cassandraproject.org)

Nonprofit, grassroots organization. Extensive documentation, links, and a focus on community preparation that is both unique and critically important. Paloma O'Riley is making a great contribution.

Impact of the Year 2000 Problem
(www.erols.com/steve451/main-y2k.htm)

When you want to analyze Y2K city/county government, this site maintained by Steve Davis, Montgomery County Budget Office, can't be beat.

Electric Utilities and Year 2000 (www.eny.2k.com)

The nation's premier authority on Y2K and the electrical utilities is Rick Cowles. This is our nation's core infrastructure, and this is the prime site to follow that concern.

Preparing for the Year 1999 Crash (www.prepare4y2k.com/index.html)

The programmer Scott Olmstead has developed one of the better personal sites and offers his commentary frequently. He was recently featured in a Wired magazine expose on Y2K. A programmer preparing for the worst possibilities.

Computer Professionals for Social Responsibility (www.cpsr.org/program/y2K)

The CPSR Y2K Working Group is ably chaired by Norman Kurland. Visit this site for all manner of useful material and subscribe to their list server for Y2K discussions.

Year 2000 Paul Revere Community Alert (www.ourworld.compuserve.com/homepages/roleigh-martin/index.htm)

Roleigh Martin provides invaluable general information, insight on embedded systems, other Y2K issues, and an excellent list of links.

Y2K Chaos (www.y2k.chaos.com)

A Christian Y2K Website. Readily understood orientation to the problem and suggested action steps. For those who see Y2K as a survival issue, a wide variety of relevant information is provided. (For a list of other Christian-oriented Y2K sites, see www.shilhavy.com/Y2K/ChristianSites.htm.)

Y2K for Women (www.y2kwomen.com)

Fills a special niche in that it is uniquely addressed to women and their emerging Y2K concerns and actions. Karen Anderson's practical counsel is much needed.

President's Council on Year 2000 Conversion (www.y2k.gov/nonjava/index.htm)

The view from the White House. Valuable links to Y2K information in every economic sector.

General Accounting Office (http://www.gas.gov/Y2K.htm)

The Y2K Congressional Watchdog site.

Senator Bennet's Year 2000 Site (http://www.senate.gov/~ bennett)

Ongoing Senate Y2K hearings.

National Association of State Information Resource Executives (NASIRE) (www.nasire.org)

Want to find out about your state government? NASIRE is an association for state-information executives. Many interesting articles and surveys on Y2K and government. To find those states that have a Y2K website for their citizens, go to state search (www.nasire.org/ss/ST2000.html).

Global Millenium Foundation (http://www.globalmf.org)
The premier Canadian site.

Institute of Electrical Engineers (http://www.iee.org.uk/2000.risk)
Best site on embedded systems.

RX2000 Solutions Institute (http://www.rx2000.org)
What's happening in the healthcare industry.

Products and Services

A. M. Leonard, Tools for the Serious Gardener
Piqua, Ohio 45356
800–543–8955; Fax 800–433–0633
Website: www.amleo.com

Innovative and earth-friendly products for serious gardeners.

Alternative Energy Engineering
Redway, California 95560
800–777–6609
Website: www.alt-energy.com
E-mail: energy@alt-energy.com

Distributors of photovoltaic, wind, and hydroelectric equipment. Catalogue and technical support available.

The Ark Institute
Monkton, Maryland 21111
800–255–1912
Website: www.lis.ab.ca/walton/geri1.html
E-mail: arkinst@concentric.net

Extensive resource for seeds and publications for "ark building."

Backwoods Solar Electric Systems
Sandpoint, Idaho 83864
208–263–4290

Exactly what it says.

Cabelas Hunting, Fishing & Outdoor Gear
Sidney, Nebraska 69160
800–237–4444; Fax: 800–496–6329

Supplier of outdoor gear.

Campmor
Saddle River, New Jersey 07458
800–226–7667

Supplier of camping equipment, clothing, and first-aid supplies.

China Diesel Imports
Jamul, California 91935
619–669–1995

Source for diesel generators.

Coleman Company
Wichita, Kansas 67219
800–835–3278

The manufacturer of the Coleman lanterns, stoves, and so on. Call for location of nearest distributor.

Dixie, U.S.A., Inc.
Houston, Texas 77255
800–233–3668
www.dixiediner.com
E-mail: info@dixieusa.com

Source for more textured vegetable protein (TVP) than you ever knew existed. And it's kosher.

Emergency Essentials
Orem, Utah 84058
800–999–1863
Website: www.beprepared.com

MREs, food, water, candles, year supply of basic foods.

Field Trips
Fergus Falls, Minnesota 56537
800–500–9266

Some interesting gear for outdoors at some very competitive prices.

Gardener's Supply Company
Burlington, Vermont 05401
800–863–1700; Fax: 800–551–6712
Website: www.gardeners.com
E-mail: info@gardeners.com

One of the most extensive supply catalogues for organic gardening. And they have a showroom.

Gaiam, Inc., dba Harmony
Broomfield, Colorado 80021
800–869–3446; Fax 800–456–1139

Very large selection of earth-friendly goods from clothing to laundry detergent to flourescent bulbs. One of the most courteous, knowledgeable, and helpful customer-service groups around. And they stand behind their products and their guarantees.

Johnny's Selected Seeds
Albion, Maine 04910
207–437–4301; Fax: 800–437–4290
Website: wwwjohnnyseeds.com
E-Mail: homegarden@johnnyseeds.com

Seed heaven. Nonhybrids. Also gardening equipment and books.

Kansas Wind Power
Holton, Kansas 66436
785–364–4407

Catalogue of independent power systems and energy efficient products. Source for solar-powered radios and short wave radios.

Kubota Tractor Corporation
Torrance, California 90503
310–370–3370

Another source for diesel generators.

L. L. Bean
Freeport, Maine 04033
800–221–4221
Website: www.llbean.com

· *World-famous supplier of all camping supplies, clothing, equipment. Stands by their merchandise. Excellent team of knowledgeable customer service people—bar none.*

Lehman's None-Electric Supply
Kidron, Ohio 44636
330–857–5757; Fax: 330–857–5785
Website: www.lehmans.com
$3.00 for catalogue
E-Mail: GetLehmans@aol.com

The be-all and end-all of nonelectric suppliers. Extensive selection of oil and gas lamps, wood and gas stoves, canning supplies, farming implements, cheese presses, composting toilets, propane refrigerators, children's toys, and a wide selection of "how-to" books. Honest and helpful customer service. It doesn't get any better than this.

Major Surplus and Survival
Gardena, California 90248
800–441–8855; Fax: 310–324–6909

Wide selection of survival gear, food, books, and so on.

Nitro-Pak Preparedness Center
Heber, Utah 84032
800–866–4876; Fax: 435–654–3860

Large selection of survival goods. Excellent service. Good source for Mountain House dehydrated foods.

Real Goods
Ukiah, California 95482
800–762–7325; Fax: 800–508–2342
Website: realgoods.com
E-mail: realgoods@realgoods.com

Wide selection of alternative energy, self-care, gardening, and solar products.

Safe-Trek Outfitters
Bozeman, Montana 59715
800–424–7870; Fax: 406–586–4842
No Website.

Very fine selection of survival goods. Their catalogue is extensive and in color.

Seed Savers Exchange
Decorah, Iowa 52101
319–382–5990; Fax: 319–382–5872

The Survival Center
McKenna, Washington 98558
800–321–2900; Fax: 800–458–6868
Website: www.zyz.com/survivalcenter
$5.00 for catalogue
E-mail: sales@survival center.com

More survival gear. Responsive people.

The Sportsman's Guide
So. St. Paul, Minnesota 55075
800–888–3006

More gear and gizmos.

Travel Smith
Novato, California 94949
800–950–1600; Fax: 800–950–1656

Some clothing that could be useful even without Y2K, and not extravagantly priced.

Urban Farming Source Book Catalogue
Bloomington, Indiana 47404
800–274–9676; Fax: 800–316–1264
Website: www.wormsway.com

These people make gardening easy even for apartment dwellers.

Vermont Country Store & Apothecary
Weston, Vermont 05255
802–362–2400; Fax 802–362–0285

Sort of a general store in a catalogue. Some hard-to-find items.

Whatever Works
Brooklyn, New York 11232
800–499–6757; Fax: 800–499–1005

Ingenious things that help with gardening and everyday living.

Don't forget your local Walmart, Sam's Club, food warehouses, kitchen stores, hardware stores, and pharmacies. Watch the newspaper for estate sales and auctions. Visit garage sales.

A magazine we found especially useful is *American Survival Guide* (800–999–9718) in Orange County, California. Phone for a subscription. Also, *Backwoods Home Magazine* (800–835–2418) in Montague, California.

The National Rifle Association has several publications that are of use. They are *American Guardian, American Hunter,* and *American Rifleman.* Among other things, the NRA is able to put you in contact with local training courses for the safe handling of firearms. Call 800–672–3888 for general information and membership.

Index

Acknowledgments

I wish to thank a number of people without whose support this book would not be in print: first, John Westergaard, Adam Kaplan, John Yellig, and the Y2K columnists on the *Westergaard Year 2000* webzine. Had it not been for John Westergaard's investing in the creation of this Website and his encouragement to do a column on Y2K issues in state and local governments, I would not have been led to understand the issues that made this book possible.

Second, I thank the dozens of public and private politicians, executives, programmers, commentators, and community activists who have expanded my awareness and enriched my understanding. And I am grateful to my column readers, who have probed my thinking and added facts and insights.

Third, my gratitude goes to the Board of Directors of the Center for Civic Renewal, who understood that public-policy improvements are possible only if the strength of our civil infrastructure is protected from damage by the century-date rollover and who encouraged me to devote a portion of my time to raising public awareness and encouraging governmental action.

Fourth, my thanks to Linda Cunningham, Publisher of HarperResource, and Lois Brown, the *Y2K* editor.

Fifth, my thanks to Alma Guinness, friend, editor, and associate, whose critical questions, original suggestions, and exceptional command of language have made this a far, far better book than it would have been without her candor and skill.

Finally, my thanks to Lois, my wife, who has shared this adventure in learning with me as a fellow researcher and whose extensive skills and knowledge have found their way onto virtually every page of this book.

About the Author

Victor W. Porlier is the executive director of the Center for Civic Renewal in New York City. He has a weekly Y2K column, called "Digital States and Associations," on the *Westergaard Year 2000* Website (www.Y2Ktimebomb.com). As Chief of Information Systems Development for the U.S. Foreign Aid Program (Agency for International Development) in the late sixties, he has been aware of the millenium bug since its early years and has been actively trying to bring the problem to the attention of the public and the nation's leaders for the past several years.